HOW TO
MAKE SPACE

HOW TO
MAKE SPACE

*An inspired guide to
a clearer mind and home*

Lona Eversden & Dr. Arlene K. Unger

Illustrations by Joanne Parry

WHITE LION
PUBLISHING

CONTENTS

A MORE SPACIOUS LIFE

We live in an age when – theoretically, at least – we have more leisure and more freedom than ever before. Yet many of us do not seem to be making the most of it. We feel stressed, overworked, forever on the go. Even our downtime seems to be filled with commitments of one sort or another: social engagements, chores, hobbies and travels. And of course, the digital revolution means that we are always connected to others: we can never really escape the madding crowd.

If you long for more room in your busy existence, this book is for you. It shows you how to create space in every aspect of your life, and so promote greater feelings of well-being and calm. Because it is only when we clear our minds and lives of unnecessary clutter, that new and wonderful things can happen. We are like flowers planted in a pot that is too small: there is only so much growing they can do until their roots need to spread further and deeper.

Space, in the broadest sense of the word, is the key to personal growth. The idea of space can be applied to many different aspects of life: the home, which we often cram with possessions and clutter; our bodies, which we allow to grow tense and constricted; our minds, which can teem with thoughts and worries; our calendars, which are often so jam-packed with plans that we have no time to nurture ourselves.

All these aspects are related. When you make space in one area of your life, you find that there is a beneficial effect elsewhere.

*'Manifest plainness, embrace simplicity,
reduce selfishness, have few desires.'*

LAO TZU

For example, when we stand upright and breathe deeply or stretch out, we find that we create spaciousness in the mind. When we tidy our living areas, that often leads to a kind of mental relief, a sudden ability to think more clearly. Like the vast expanding universe, space creates more space as it grows.

A World of Wisdom

An awareness of a need for space goes back to the beginnings of society. People from all cultures and civilizations have developed rituals and customs, sayings and traditions that emphasize the need for space in our lives in order to promote well-being and happiness. This book introduces you to the different expressions of that wisdom through fifty myths and legends, festivals, spiritual traditions and folk customs, ideas or works of art that celebrate or facilitate the human need for freedom, expansion, exploration and spaciousness. We look at symbols drawn from nature – the horizon, or the butterfly; spiritual beliefs from the Ancient Egyptians, Romans and Celts; mores and manners from

Scandinavia to Japan, teachings from Buddhism to Taoism; and the work of artists and poets whose particular gift is to tap into the deep well of human consciousness.

Use this collection of stories and exercises in whatever way suits you best. Open the book at any page and find something to interest, encourage and support you, or read it through from start to finish, perhaps working on a different exercise each week. Or select the chapter that deals with the aspect of life that you most want to work on – the home, time, the mind, or the body – and see which ideas and exercises feel most appealing or relevant. Every generation has distilled its special wisdom and passed it down to us. Open the book as you might open a door and let the light flood in. A new sense of freedom and spaciousness is within your grasp.

*'Happiness is a place between too
little and too much.'*

FINNISH PROVERB

'*I am looking forward enormously
to getting back to the sea again, where the
overstimulated psyche can recover in
the presence of that infinite peace
and spaciousness.*'

CARL JUNG

CHAPTER ONE:
SPACE AT HOME

'The real cost of keeping things is the
amount of thought you put in their keeping.
[...] In this way does this, the blind desire
of mere keeping and hoarding, keep many
people poor, and even makes paupers.'

PRENTICE MULFORD

AN OPEN DOOR

'When one door closes, another opens.'

ALEXANDER GRAHAM BELL

The front door of a home is the ultimate symbol of personal space. The first constructed and closable doors (as opposed to mere openings in walls) were used by the Ancient Egyptians. They put simple wooden doors on dwellings and also built highly decorative false doors on the walls of tombs to allow the souls of the dead to pass through to the underworld. The Romans perfected the technology of the door – building them from metal and adding hinges and locking mechanisms. They also invented a god of doorways and thresholds, Janus, who looks both backwards and forwards at the same time.

Janus, God of the Doorway

The first month of the Roman calendar – January – is named after Janus, an indication of his significance in the Roman pantheon. He is represented with two heads facing in opposite directions, so that he might watch over both the outside and inside of a home. According to the Roman poet Ovid, Janus's temple doors were left closed in times of peace, lest the peace should escape, and open during war so it might enter once more. As well as doorways, Janus ruled over journeys and beginnings – because every beginning is like opening a door onto a new and undiscovered room, and every journey carries us across a threshold into a new space.

FIRST IMPRESSIONS

We all look forward to arriving home after a long day at the office, being stuck in bumper-to-bumper traffic or doing last minute errands. But does the physical entrance to your home provide the warm welcome we crave, making us feel like we are stepping into a cosy, warm and calm abode? Here are some practical tips to make the entranceway to your home a welcoming area reflective of the environment we want to foster inside:

Keep it simple   Believe it or not, keeping things simple and clean can make your home appear more inviting. No one wants to walk into an entryway that is cluttered and untidy.

A lighter side   Have fun with lighting. Lamps and candles not only add a warm ambience but positive energy to a space.

Bright and happy   Splash some colour in your entryway. You don't have to paint the area to achieve this — a wall hanging, some art or even a colourful vase can give a pop of mood-raising bright. Adding such touches makes the bold statement that this home is full of life and art.

Ring the bell   The sound of a pleasant doorbell can be a wonderful greeting to someone who has just come from noisy traffic or a busy day. You could also try placing some wind chimes by the doorway to add a calming sound to welcome guests on arrival.

Smells like home   Smells can hold powerful memories of place. Make the association with your home the most pleasant you can by placing a home fragrance diffuser or scented candle near the entrance. Bouquets of fresh flowers are also a lovely way to naturally scent a space.

Add texture   What about a lovely rug? A durable soft fabric over your entryway floor is not only welcoming but practical for this area of heavy foot traffic.

Bring the outside in   Plants and natural items such as shells or driftwood can provide a relaxed ambience. It is also a nice way to bring some of your favourite elements of the outside world in to your home.

MORE BANG FOR YOUR BUCK

Giving your entranceway the ambience and personality that reflects your style of living doesn't have to cost a fortune. Consider visiting second-hand shops or repurposing old bottles, metal containers or frames to create decorative touches that can lift the space.

IN WITH THE NEW

Our ancestors felt the seasons much more keenly than we do. They longed for the warmth of spring and for its longer days after the cold, inhospitable months of winter. So it's not surprising that the spring is celebrated all over the world. In India, this takes the form of the vibrant festival of Holi, in which revellers fling handfuls of colourful powders over each other. In Mexico people flock to visit the Mayan ruins of Chichén Itzá, where the stepped main pyramid (El Castillo) was built at such an angle that during the spring and autumn equinoxes the sun casts a shadow that appears like a serpent slithering down the steps. The Iranian festival of Nowruz also takes place at the spring equinox and marks the Persian New Year. Over thirteen days of festivities, people visit each other's homes and exchange gifts before spending the last day of celebration outdoors in nature.

A Season for Change

In various cultures, the spring festival is preceded by a deep clean of the home space. In Nowruz, this tradition is called 'shaking the house' and involves dusting and beating furniture and curtains. The Chinese traditionally sweep their houses from top to bottom in order to rid them of bad luck before New Year, which is celebrated in spring, and Jewish people also spend the days before Passover cleansing their homes.

   The tradition of cleaning every corner of the home in the days before Passover relates to the Biblical story of the escape of the

Israelites from slavery in Egypt, which the festival commemorates. According to the Bible, the Israelites – led by Moses – left in such haste that their bread did not have time to rise, so during the days of Passover no leavened food is eaten. Spring cleaning ensures that any stray crumbs of *chametz*, leavened food, are removed from the home before the festival.

SPRING CLEANING

In earlier times, spring cleaning offered city dwellers the chance to fling open the windows and clear the home of soot that had accumulated from the fireplace over the winter months. But, even in modern times, the annual deep clean will help you to enjoy your space more. Here's how to go about it:

1. Get all your supplies together before you start. Put everything you need – rubber gloves, clothes, scrubbers, cleaning liquids – in a bucket so it is easy to transport.
2. Start at the top and work downwards. This goes for the home in general and also for each room – start with the lighting fixtures and do the floor last. Generally speaking, tidy first, then dust and then clean.
3. Expect to spend several days spring cleaning. Try tackling the job in sections – perhaps one floor at a time, or do the bedrooms, then the bathrooms, then the living space, followed by the kitchen.
4. Time yourself. To keep on track, decide how long you want to spend on a particular area – thirty minutes, say – and set a timer. For the period you have chosen, focus all your energies on cleaning.
5. Enlist support. If you live with other people, get them involved in the cleaning too – children as well. If you all work at the same time then you will see fast progress.

Hire help if you need to – many cleaning companies offer a one-off deep-clean service.

6. Sort out your spring-clean playlist. Cleaning is more fun when you are listening to some upbeat music.

7. Don't forget to sort your clothes out. Take heavy winter coats and the like to the dry cleaners, ready for next year. If there are clothes you won't be wearing for a while, put them in sealed bags (with moth balls) and remove to the attic or other storage space to make room for spring and summer clothing.

A JOB A DAY

Write yourself a list of thirty jobs you need to do occassionally to keep your home looking sparkling – cleaning the windows, wiping out kitchen cupboards, cleaning the extractor fan, descaling the kettle, tidying the linen cupboard or drawer, vacuuming your mattress. Do one job per day throughout the month, and tick it off when you have finished.

NEGATIVE SPACE

*'The green reed which bends in the wind is stronger than
the mighty oak which breaks in a storm.'*

CONFUCIUS

I n traditional Chinese brush painting, bamboo appears as a
subject over and over again. Ancient bamboo paintings were
created using the strokes of calligraphy — with the greatest masters
priding themselves on using minimal lines to create exquisite
images. Many images show a single stalk of bamboo and much of
their beauty is in the fact that the bamboos are surrounded by space
— there is no sense of crowding or clutter around them. The same
principle applies in the three-dimensional spaces of our homes:
we need to give as much attention to the empty areas as we do to
arranging the things that we own. Empty space often adds more
value to our lives than yet another object. If you want to reduce the
clutter content of your home, try this exercise:

1. Get two bags — one for rubbish and one for giving away
   — and take them to the space you want to clear.
2. Go through each item in the area and ask yourself:
   Do I love it?
   Do I need it?
   Have I used it in the last twelve months?
   Is it more valuable than the space it is taking?

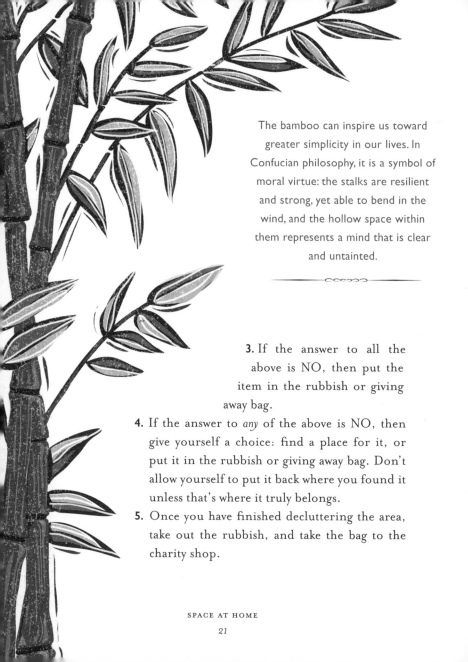

The bamboo can inspire us toward greater simplicity in our lives. In Confucian philosophy, it is a symbol of moral virtue: the stalks are resilient and strong, yet able to bend in the wind, and the hollow space within them represents a mind that is clear and untainted.

3. If the answer to all the above is NO, then put the item in the rubbish or giving away bag.

4. If the answer to *any* of the above is NO, then give yourself a choice: find a place for it, or put it in the rubbish or giving away bag. Don't allow yourself to put it back where you found it unless that's where it truly belongs.

5. Once you have finished decluttering the area, take out the rubbish, and take the bag to the charity shop.

CURATE YOUR LIFE

*'Have nothing in your home that you do not know to
be useful or believe to be beautiful.'*
WILLIAM MORRIS

The Victorian designer and artist William Morris believed that the home should be a reflection of its owners's personality, as well as a pleasing space to occupy. His own home, the Red House, became a living expression of his artistic ideas. One room led to another, creating a sense of flow that was very different from the traditional Victorian home. Huge windows allowed light to flood in, creating a sense of openness and space. And every aspect — from the furnishings to the art — was selected to enhance daily life. Tastes have changed, but Morris's principles remain pertinent for modern living. Follow these five simple principles for a more spacious living environment:

1. Have things in your home that you find lovely to look at — art, well-crafted furniture, thoughtful objects.
2. Go for simple shapes without fussy details. Curved shapes are more natural and more conducive to rest and relaxation than lots of angles and straight lines.
3. Give your treasures room to breathe. One or two objects on a shelf tend to look better than a crowd.
4. Create flow: Morris's own house was designed so that one space flowed seamlessly into the next,

creating a more harmonious home and impression of greater spaciousness.

5. Throw out the bad. Morris advised, 'if you cannot learn to love real art; at least learn to hate sham art and reject it.' We all have things in our homes that are badly made or ugly in some way — perhaps gifts that we feel we cannot get rid of or things that we bought as a stopgap. If there is something in your home that you dislike, get rid of it.

LESS IS MORE

'He has the most who is most content with the least.'

DIOGENES OF SINOPE

O ne of the key concepts in the philosophy of minimalism is this: if you want to make space, have less. It echoes the thinking of many ancient philosophers – including Diogenes of Sinope and the Roman thinker Seneca – who advocated a life of simplicity and self-sufficiency. More than 2,000 years later, these theories are gaining wider attention as many people start to challenge the competitive consumerism of the modern world. In some parts of the world we now have the capacity to buy more things than ever before. At the same time, we are coming to the realization that possessions do not make us happy. Indeed, a large body of recent research has found that excessive consumption is actually related to lower well-being.

Ancient Wisdom

Many legends have grown up around the life of Diogenes of Sinope, the Greek advocate of self-sufficiency and simple morality. Exiled from his hometown, Diogenes embraced a life of poverty in Athens. He deliberately reduced his needs to the bare minimum, partly as a way of highlighting the lavish excess of Athenian society. He would sleep wherever he could find a space in order to show that a man could be happy whatever his circumstances. One story tells how, after seeing a boy drink from cupped hands, he threw

away his sole possession, a wooden bowl. 'Fool that I am,' he said, 'to have been carrying unnecessary baggage all this time.' Most of us could not go that far, but Diogenes' attitude can help inspire us to reduce what we buy, and to live in a simpler, more spacious way.

MINDFUL SHOPPING

In the last thirty years, the development of data analytics and information sharing has meant that we have become more vulnerable to consumer marketing tactics. Often, these are so ingrained in everyday life that we aren't even aware that we are being sold something. Here is simple exercise to practice mindful shopping and encourage conscious consumerism rather than impulse buying. Practise this when you are overloaded by information to help you stay true to your needs and not get swept up in manufactured wants.

1. Mindful shopping (in store or online) begins with a plan. Write down what you need or are specifically looking to purchase. Rank the items in order of necessity, and consider discarding those things that are low priorities.

2. Now come up with a realistic amount of time to give yourself to browse or purchase each item, whether you are browsing in store or on the internet.

3. Before heading out or logging on to your device, commit to a realistic budget to spend. Knowing what you can comfortably afford and sticking to it takes the guess work out of shopping and reduces the chance of impulse buying.

4. As you walk to the shops or start browsing online, recognize that breaks are important. Consider taking

a mindful brain break every fifteen minutes. This is important before you finally make the purchase.

5. Having browsed for a while and stuck to your plan, find a quiet place to sit down. Your cart might be full, but take a moment reflect on the day or let your mind wander. Whatever your recollection might be, this will change your focus for a few minutes and help you regain objectivity.

6. Ask yourself if you really need what you are about to purchase? Could you wait or make it on your own?

7. If you still want to make the purchase, before you pay for it make sure it is a price you can easily afford.

8. Driving home with your item, or when away from the computer, check in with yourself on how well you did. Do you still feel good about the purchase? Are you going to use it or give it away? Were you proud of how you executed your plan? What would you do differently next time?

9. If all went according to plan, take a moment to reward yourself. This could be by sharing the news about your purchase with a friend or loved one, enjoying a cup of tea or running a calming bath.

COLOUR CODE

'The deeper the blue becomes the more strongly it calls man towards the infinite.'

WASSILY KANDINSKY

B ecause it is the colour of the boundless skies, blue is the colour most often associated with spaciousness and the infinite. The Egyptians painted the ceilings of their tombs in deep blue scattered with gold stars, and Krishna, the Hindu god of compassion, is often depicted with blue skin – compassion, after all, is openness to all the suffering that exists under the vault of heaven.

Distant objects, such as mountains, take on a blue cast – so we instinctively associate blue with wide, open landscapes. It creates a sense of openness and calm, because – as Kandinsky sensed – it is the colour of infinity. Here are some simple ways to make the most of this calming colour in your home:

1. Use light colours from the cool end of the spectrum to make a small area seem bigger. Blue seems to draw the eye toward it and can create a greater sense of space than other hues.

2. Paint your ceiling a lighter shade than the walls to make it appear higher. In general, keep the darkest shades near to the floor to add to the illusion of space.

3. Blue is said to slow the heartbeat, so is particularly good for rooms where you want to feel relaxed – it's often used in bedrooms and bathrooms for this reason.

4. Blue can be a little chilly-looking so be sure to balance it with some warmer colours. Blue's complement is orange, which makes a bright contrast, but if you want a softer look go for warm browns and terracottas.

The German poet Johann Wolfgang von Goethe was fascinated by the emotional impact of colour. His colour wheel spaced the colours according to principles of chromatic harmony: he divided the spectrum into warm and cool colours, suggesting that warm colours such as red and yellow were energizing and uplifting, while cool hues were draining and depressing. His ideas greatly influenced artists such as J. M. W. Turner and, later, Wassily Kandinsky.

FOOD, FRIENDS AND CONVERSATION

The table is a space that invites people to gather, eat, share. Communal eating – something that our ancestors would have done out of necessity – still chimes deep within our souls providing a space for nurturing relationships, as well as sharing ideas and conversation. Research suggests that the more often people eat together, the greater their life satisfaction and happiness.

Gather Round

In the Middle Ages most tables were rectangular, with the top of the table a place of honour and precedence. But in the legend of the mythical British King Arthur, he and his knights are said to have gathered around a large round table – so not one knight, or king for that matter, was seated higher than another.

A symbol of knightly ideals, in the Middle Ages round tables were made for royal feasts and, throughout Europe, there were jousting tournaments called 'round tables' in Arthur's honour. Even now, we refer to 'round-table discussions', meaning that all participants are equal and every opinion expressed is to be taken into account. Whether we are talking or eating, the round table stands for fellowship and community, and is a reminder of the importance of creating spaces within our homes – and workplaces – where people can come together to share ideas, swap stories, and develop the human bonds that are essential to well-being.

OUR HOUSE

Just as in the days of King Arthur, the home is a place where family members, friends and room-mates need to feel supported and respected. Fostering a sense of cohesion in your home is a two-fold task: it requires delicate structuring as well as quality time. Here are some practical ways for you to foster community and togetherness in the home:

Bring warmth into your home Gathering around a fireplace or a cosy rug brings out laughter, human honesty and an unspoken sense of belonging in everyone. Warm focal points such as a fire or rug set the scene for stories to be told and games to be played.

A place for everyone People feel more respected, as well as connected, when they have defined places in the home. Have family members got their favourite spots? Is there enough seating in the common living areas for all the family and guests? Table size is another consideration, especially since this the key piece of furniture around which people commune. When everyone feels there is room for them around the table, people feel cohesive and conversant, and not left out.

Food attracts Whether it's meal time or not, having healthy snacks to nibble on the coffee table or on the kitchen side will certainly draw a crowd. People love to congregate where there are snacks and catch up on the news of the day.

Practicality over perfection A comfortable couch where everyone can kick back is preferred over one that you are afraid to get stained or even use. Make sure to design your space for living.

Be house proud Everyone deserves to enjoy a nicely decorated home; there is so much you can do to give your home character with simple touches. It's also easier to keep a decorated home clean and comfortable than dealing with old or tattered furniture and unloved spaces.

Say no to noise pollution If you want to promote lively discussion among family members, rethink how much noise is coming from your television or Xbox. People are more likely break the silence with questions and chatter when there is no background noise. Living in a home where the television is constantly on tends to lead to less interaction and more isolation.

COME TOGETHER

Interior designers recommend keeping seating in living areas relatively close together to create a welcoming atmosphere. Furniture placed further apart or separated by other objects can lead to guests feeling removed from one another.

COSY COMFORT

'Surely everyone is aware of the divine pleasures which attend a wintry fireside.'

THOMAS DE QUINCEY

I n Norway, especially in the far north, the sun remains hidden for months at a stretch during the winter. But rather than dreading the cold season, many people celebrate it as a time to enjoy their homes, using their indoor spaces as a retreat from the harsh elements. This approach is encapsulated in the philosophy of *koselig* – loosely translated as 'cosy', but really a word used to describe the warm, happy feeling you get inside when doing pleasing things. Here are four ways to create a positive winter mindset by getting *koselig*:

1. **Light candles** Few things are more *koselig* than a lit candle, so use them all around your home. Arrange candles in groups of three or five to create a warm and inviting light in your living spaces. Enjoy the flickering flames of a real fire, too, if you have one; otherwise make sure that your home is well insulated and heated.

2. **Snuggle up** Soft blankets and throws are a must for feeling *koselig*, so have these to hand in your living space. Choose warm colours such as red, orange and amber. And invest in good slippers.

3. **Draw in** It's traditional to hang out with a smaller group of people in winter – family or a few close

friends — and to socialize in people's homes rather than battling through deep snow to restaurants and bars. So, if you want to be *koselig*, feel free to turn down party invites in favour of more intimate gatherings and feeling homely.

4. **Be active** Being *koselig* doesn't mean getting sluggish. Wrapping up warm and going for a bracing hike before returning to your snug warm space is exactly the spirit of the word. Shared activities at home are also part of this wintry Scandinavian way of being: in Norway, a perfect evening might involve playing board games or sharing cooking skills with people you love.

HUNKER DOWN

Every animal has its own space, a place where it can feel safe and rest. Birds and many mammals spend much time and energy building their homes, but few have as organized a home as the groundhog. This animal — which, according to folklore can predict whether the winter will be long or short — is an impressive tunneller. It digs an elaborate burrow that can be up to twenty meters long and have several chambers. Among the groundhog's 'rooms' are a special space for hibernating, as well as a summer burrow and even a bathroom area.

Spring Watch

Groundhog Day is celebrated on 2 February in the United States — notably in Punxsutawney, Pennsylvania. People gather to watch as a groundhog comes out of its burrow to see if it is time to end its hibernation. If the skies are clear and the groundhog sees a shadow on the ground, this is said to mean a longer winter and the groundhog continues its rest; if, however, the skies are cloudy and there is no shadow, then spring is near and it can end its sleep.

In Ireland, there is a similar tradition, but the forecasting animal was a hedgehog, and in Germany the equivalent was *dachstag*, or 'day of the badger'. Whatever the animal, nature's hibernators instinctively know when to rest and when to re-engage with the world. We can draw inspiration from their example, reminding ourselves of the importance of creating a warm and cosy space where we can sleep deeply and restore our spirits.

A PLACE OF REST

An animal's home, carefully constructed and lovingly maintained, has become a broader symbol of homeliness, caring and nurturing. Burrows inspire us to imagine spaces of safety and restfulness — particularly calling to mind the bedroom, a place of sanctuary, intimacy and relaxation within our homes. Creating a serene refuge that promotes restfulness is vital as studies show that we need restorative sleep for our mental alertness, emotional stability and physical well-being. Try these tips:

Ditch the devices   In order to ensure that we get a good night sleep our bodies need to produce natural melatonin. Unfortunately, our electronic devices interfere with that process, as both the messages and the blue light emitted disrupt our minds preparing for rest. Consider leaving your last-minute texts, emails and games for daylight hours.

Smell the roses   Psychological research has found that a pleasant floral scent puts us in a better frame of mind and mood. Think of a favourite fragrance that you'd like to add to your nightstand. Putting out a scented candle, diffuser, a fresh bouquet or lavender oil scent can set the scene for a more restful snooze.

Remember the good times   Scientists from University of California, Berkeley, discovered that we can switch to a happier state of mind just by looking at fond memories. Displaying a few of your treasured photos by your bedside might help to ensure more pleasant images and dreams as you fall asleep.

Form habits Night rituals, such as turning down a made bed, can ensure a more restful night's sleep. A routine of cleaning your bedroom, preparing for sleep and making your bed will contribute to your bedroom's calm atmosphere.

Colour coordinate According to research from the University of British Columbia, soft pastels, especially blue, are most soothing in the bedroom, while sticking with natural colours, such as a light green, reminds of us of nature. Painting your bedroom walls these colours can put you in a more uplifting mood.

Curve appeal Curves are not only cool but calming, according to psychological design research. Adding more rounded edges to your bedroom décor can calm your nerves and boost your happiness quotient. The next time you are looking for bedroom furnishings, consider softer geometric lines to foster a relaxing bedroom atmosphere.

Keep it clean Numerous psychological studies have shown a strong association between depression and clutter. Making your bedroom clutter-free can promote relaxation and reduce stress.

SOWING SEEDS

B y its nature, a garden is an enclosed space, which serves as our own private sanctuary as well as connecting us to nature and the elements. The earliest gardens are likely to have been practical spaces — orchards and vegetable patches — but archaeological evidence tells us that trees and plants were used to enhance human habitations as long as 6,000 years ago. In one Egyptian tomb a wooden model of a garden was found; it consisted of a still pool surrounded by delicately carved trees. And there are many writings that refer to that miracle of architecture and horticulture — the hanging gardens of Babylon.

The Hanging Gardens of Babylon

Mystery surrounds the whereabouts of the fabled Hanging Gardens of Babylon — one of the Seven Wonders of the World. One story holds that they were created by King Nebuchadrezzar II, who ruled the city of Babylon in modern-day Iraq, around 600 BCE. The tall tiered gardens, replete with trees and shrubs, were a gift for his beloved wife Amytis who pined for the lush green mountains of her homeland. But the gardens may not have been in Babylon at all. Some believe that the legend refers to tiered gardens in Nineveh, where the Assyrian king boasted of having created 'a wonder for all people' in his palace and gardens. Wherever the gardens were — even if they are in fact a myth — they remain a testament to the human desire to create beauty in the outdoors: physical spaces of calm that allow our mind to clear and time to recede.

GREEN FINGERS

Gardens can be the happiest space, a room open to the skies and furnished with flowers. The act of tending a garden reminds us of the continual possibility of growth and renewal, which can have psychological benefits. In the gentlest of ways, immersing ourselves in nature and interacting with it provides a sense that we are not the centre of the world, that life continues whatever our personal moods. This awareness can be very healing, because it encourages us to look outward rather than inward, and so attain a sense of mental as well as physical space. To make the most of even a small garden, try these ideas:

Go vertical   Use trees or shrubs that are columnar in shape so they don't take up too much of your garden's 'footprint'. Climbing plants help draw the eye upwards and an organic curtain of green helps to soften the harsh boundaries of a fence or wall, making a space look bigger. If you have a tiny outdoor area, use raised beds. Or stack a series of planters of decreasing size one on top of each other (like a mini hanging garden) to create vertical interest and maximise the greenery within the space.

Use mirrors   Well-placed mirrors can create the illusion of a window into another, more distant, garden, or you can use them to reflect light into shady corners. A mirror will look more natural if it is surrounded by plants rather than standing starkly alone. Make sure that the view in the reflection is one of greenery.

GET A GARDENER'S BOOST

Many studies have attested to the benefits of gardening. One project by the universities of Essex and Westminster found that thirty minutes' gardening a week was enough to help improve self-esteem and mood. If you don't have a garden, you can gain the same benefits from working on an allotment – or start small with a window box or mini-container garden.

Declutter Just as an excess of furniture makes an indoor space look smaller, so too does garden paraphernalia. Keep benches, pots and tools to a minimum, and tidy away items when not in use.

Use pale hues Choose garden furniture in white or pale wood, and paint the surrounding walls in white to create an airy feel.

Go large This may sound counterintuitive, but it's better to stock your garden with generously leaved plants rather than sticking to those with small foliage, which can add to the sense of clutter.

Choose monochrome Sticking to flowers of one colour helps to create a sense of unity and reduce any sense of visual clutter.

Have a sit spot Make sure that you have a place to sit and enjoy your garden. Make a point of spending time here, breathing in and enjoying your beautiful space.

COMING HOME

'Home is where the heart is.'
ENGLISH PROVERB

Mythology and folklore abound with tales of adventurers returning joyously home from their long quest. We all recognize the idea that wherever we go, it is our home space that holds the secret to happiness. One of the most famous stories of a homeward journey is Homer's *Odyssey*, which tells how the Greek hero Odysseus was forced to wander for ten years after the Trojan war before returning at last to his home on the island of Ithaca.

The Long Way Round

In the *Odyssey*, Odysseus never wavers from his desire to return to his home and wife, the faithful Penelope. But his journey is a long and treacherous one, full of diversion and detour. In one episode, Odysseus is shipwrecked and is eventually washed up on the island of Ogygia, home to the sea nymph Calypso who falls in love with her accidental visitor and cares for him. The island is beautiful and Odysseus has everything a mortal could desire. Yet his longing to go home never abates, even after seven long years spent imprisoned in this apparent paradise. Eventually the gods intercede on his behalf and Calypso releases him. Odysseus finally makes it back to Ithaca, and to Penelope. The *Odyssey's* trials are a reminder that — in the words of another traveller through strange lands, Dorothy in *The Wizard of Oz* — 'There's no place like home'.

EVERYDAY HOMECOMING

'It is good people who make good places.'
ANNA SEWELL

Feeling at home is a basic human need. Some people can create a sense of home wherever they are, but most of us look to the places that we live in to provide us with a sense of security and belonging. A home is much more than four walls — it's the atmosphere that creates a sense of welcome. Try these ideas to help create a homecoming welcome every day.

1. When a loved one returns home, stop what you are doing and greet them - go to the door or entranceway as they arrive. If it is you who are coming home, then go and find your loved one to say hello.
2. Make eye contact as you greet each other. Hug, properly — a twenty-second hug prompts the brain to release oxytocin, the 'love hormone', which helps build feelings of connection and security.
3. Save the negatives. If you have had a bad day, try to wait a while before you offload. Have a cup of tea, get changed — do whatever you need in order to arrive home emotionally as well as physically. (See page 78 for some 'transition rituals' that will help with this.)
4. Underline the sense of greeting and welcome by creating a physical space that is pleasurable to enter.

HELLO, GOODBYE

Leave-takings are as important emotionally
as homecomings. When you go out, don't
simply shout out a hurried 'see you later',
but make space for a proper goodbye.
Greeting and farewell rituals help to
underline close family bonds and build a
sense of belonging and trust.

――――――――○○○○○○――――――――

In particular, keep your hallway or entrance area clear
– stacks of paper, piles of shoes and other clutter can
make the space harder to navigate and less appealing.

5. Smell is our most evocative sense, so create a home
aroma that is positive and pleasurable by using an
aromatherapy diffuser or candles. Lighting one as soon
as you come in for the evening can be both a pleasurable
ritual and a sensual way of improving your space.

6. Think sound. Slow, quiet music is known to have a
relaxing effect on us, so have it on in the background
when your loved ones come home. Studies show that
listening to classical music promotes the release of the
happy hormone dopamine in the brain.

CHAPTER TWO:
TAKE YOUR TIME

'Let us know the happiness time brings,
not count the years.'

AUSONIUS

˙ TICK TOCK, TICK TOCK

I'm late, I'm late... When the White Rabbit in Lewis Carroll's *Alice in Wonderland* dashes past, frantically checking his watch, he epitomizes the modern feeling that we are time-poor. Most of us feel that there is simply not the space in the day to do all the things we need to. But in reality, the present generation has more leisure than any previous one. Our problem is not that we have less time, but that we are too driven by the clock. We are so used to tracking the minutes that it is hard to imagine that people once lived in a very different way.

The Origins of the Clock

The earliest cultures had no concept of time in the sense of measured hours and minutes. The sun's progress across the sky was their only way to track the passing of the day. Advanced civilizations, such as the Babylonians and the Ancient Egyptians, developed sun dials for the day and — when the sun had set — the Egyptians used water clocks, which measured out time in slow regular drips. The Greeks refined the water clock, which they called *clepsydra*, meaning 'water thief'. The name suggests that the earliest time-keepers understood that measuring time can be a negative as well as a positive. The Greek philosopher Aristotle grumbled that 'the length of a tragedy should not be judged by the *clepsydra* but by what is suitable for the plot'. In other words, Aristotle advises that we need to focus on what really matters, rather than trying to cram things into a particular time frame.

PLAYTIME

'Time is what we want most, but what we use worst.'
WILLIAM PENN

From candle and water clocks, sun dials and hourglasses to clock towers, the grandfather clock and watches, humankind has long sought to measure time. With the pressures of modern-day life we can often feel that we don't have enough hours in the day, but it is important for our emotional well-being to set aside an hour or two each week to enjoy a fun activity. Here are some steps to effectively block out time in your hectic schedule:

1. Adopt the idea that not only is free time good for your health, but it will help you to discover who you are and to be content with your own self.
2. Think of something you have longed to do during your busy week but put on hold — like going on a hike, cycling along the ocean, taking up needle-point or reading a good thriller.
3. Say out loud the very thing that makes your soul feel like jumping for joy.
4. Now take out your diary or open your phone calendar. Find some hours where you can break away from your obligations to do that very thing: circle the day and time clearly in your diary, and make a promise to yourself that you won't postpone or reduce it.

REAP THE REWARDS

Mindfully scheduling free time not only enables us to pursue activities and pastimes that we truly enjoy, but has numerous other benefits such as boosting our productivity at work and setting priorities. It can also provide much-needed perspective on life. When we are in the middle of an important business project, it is easy for work to become all-consuming. Taking some scheduled time-out allows us to recognize that there are other aspects of our life that are equally as important and shouldn't be neglected.

5. Allow yourself to get excited about your upcoming activity by gathering the items you need, planning your route or telling friends and family about your plan.

6. After the activity, check in with yourself about how it went and what you'd do differently next time: it is your free time and you can adapt and tweak it as you like. Thank yourself for giving yourself the space and time to pursue a favourite hobby.

7. There is nothing more enriching in life than giving yourself free time to just chill out and have fun. Recognize the importance of creating space in your calendar for more fun and play, and commit to setting aside dedicated free time every week.

SIMPLE ROUTINE

Albert Einstein knew more about time than anyone, and he had a handy trick to introduce a little more of it into his day: he is said to have owned a set of identical suits so that he didn't waste time wondering what to wear. 'Everything should be as simple as possible, but not simpler,' was his mantra. All of us need to find ways to avoid 'decision fatigue', because the fewer small decisions you have to make, the better primed you will be for the big ones. Here are some other ways to streamline your decision-making first thing in the morning:

Keep food simple   When it comes to the first meal of the day, keep it straightforward and healthy. There's something soothing about having the same breakfast each day, and it means there is one less decision to make.

Dress ahead   Your clothes needn't be the same every day, of course. But you will make space in your morning if you have all your clothes ready the night before.

Do the bag drop   When you come home after work, make a point of clearing out your pockets and bag of any debris. Make sure you have everything in it that you will need the next day.

Einstein is not the only great thinker to have streamlined
his routine. Barack Obama simplified his wardrobe when
president of the United States, while Oprah combines two
tasks in one when she takes her dogs for their daily walk,
also enabling her to get outside for some fresh air.

SLOW AND STEADY

Want to make more space in your day? The answer could be to go slower. Many spiritual thinkers have noted that the more we rush, the less progress we seem to make. The most charming illustration of this point is a fable reputedly written by a Greek slave named Aesop in around 600 BCE. Aesop is said to have been a keen observer of animals and used their characters as the basis for tales with a moral message for humans. Whether Aesop even existed is a matter of a debate, but the tales that are ascribed to him are a treasure trove of ancient wisdom that has delighted readers for centuries.

Racing Ahead

In the Aesop fable 'The Tortoise and the Hare', a hare is bragging about how fast he can run. He mocks a tortoise for his slowness: 'How do you ever get anywhere?' The tortoise looks calmly at the hare and replies that he gets where he wants to go and quicker than the hare might think, and he challenges the hare to a race to prove it. Much amused, the hare accepts. The animals set off and the hare leaves the tortoise far behind in the distance – so far behind that he decides to take a rest. He soon drops off and as the hare sleeps the tortoise plods on. In time, he passes the hare, still asleep. When the hare finally wakes up, he sees the tortoise in the distance far ahead. He runs as fast he can but it's too late: the tortoise wins the race. The moral is that slow and steady beats fast and unfocussed.

SLOW YOUR DAY DOWN

'Nature does not hurry, yet everything is accomplished.'

LAO TZU

If you feel like you are constantly in a hurry, take inspiration from Aesop's tortoise and slow down. Here are some tips to beat the rushing habit:

Get up earlier than you need to   A rushed morning means starting the day frazzled.

Don't overschedule   Rather than trying to arrange meetings or complete tasks back-to-back, keep spaces in your day, so that when tasks overrun there is time to finish them off.

Mind the gap   Find a way of marking the transition between one activity and the next. Even in the busiest day, there are moments of emptiness when you can pause, breathe and appreciate life.

Leave extra time   Don't try to plan your journey to arrive somewhere exactly on time. Leave half an hour earlier than you need to, so that you can take it slowly. Find something pleasurable to do on the journey, too. Listen to a podcast or read a good book.

Get used to waiting Often we rush around because we can't bear the thought of sitting still and waiting. Aim to arrive at appointments a few minutes early and train yourself to sit calmly taking in your surroundings rather than automatically distracting yourself with your phone. It may feel uncomfortable at first but with practice you will find it easier to do this.

Know that tomorrow is another day Accept the fact that you may not achieve everything today. Many of the deadlines we give ourselves are false — does it really matter if you don't send that email or do that task? Sure, sometimes it does, but often things can wait without any disastrous consequence.

See leisure as important When you are busy, it is tempting to cut back on downtime. But downtime is what helps you regain the headspace you need to be productive and effective at work. Remind yourself how important it is to give yourself a break.

MEANINGFUL MOMENTS

R ituals are a feature of all societies and cultures. They fulfil a deep psychological and social need by taking us to a space that is outside the daily routine. In this space we can connect with our group or with our feelings — to bond, to heal, to find meaning. A ritual can be seen as a way of framing a moment for all to see: a wedding is both a private and a public declaration of love, a funeral a personal and a communal space in which to grieve. Not all rituals, though, deal with the great life events.

The Art of Tea

The Japanese tea ritual is a carefully choreographed and elongated ceremony that elevates the simple act of drinking a cup of green tea to an art form. It takes place in a room that is sparsely decorated: each item has been chosen with care and placed in a way that conveys a sense of spaciousness, openness and beauty. All participants remove their shoes before entering and wash their hands as a way of symbolically cleansing themselves of the dust of the outside world. The guests kneel on cushions and spend time taking in the atmosphere. Then the host cleans the utensils — an elaborate performance done with slow graceful movements — before preparing the tea and then serving it. At the end of the ceremony, guests admire and complement the utensils as a way of showing respect. The ritual can take up to four hours — and can transform forever the way you look at your morning cuppa.

CREATING A DAILY RITUAL

Introducing small daily rituals into your life is a wonderful way to ensure that you make space for self-care, something that can easily get squeezed out when we are busy. The Vietnamese monk Thich Nhat Hanh, who introduced mindfulness to the West, recommends meditating with a cup of tea. Try this mini mindfulness meditation to help create a calm space in your morning routine:

1. Find a pleasing space in which to drink your tea. Choose your favourite spot in your home, one that you associate with relaxation.
2. Make yourself a cup of tea and settle down to enjoy it. Have nothing else to do at this time. Switch off your phone or leave it in another room.
3. Hold the cup in both hands and allow yourself to become aware of the warmth you can feel in your palms.
4. Breathe slowly and deeply as you sit, just holding the cup, doing nothing else.
5. Slowly bring the cup up to your lips, noticing how your movements bring it to the precise place you need in order to drink.
6. Inhale softly, opening up to the aroma of the tea. There's no need to sniff it — breathe normally and notice what you can smell.

7. Then take a sip of your drink. Hold the liquid in your mouth and mark the feeling of warmth and the flavours you are experiencing.
8. Swallow the mouthful, noticing the tiny movements involved in moving the liquid to the back of the throat.
9. Take a simple breath in and out, and then repeat. See if you can enjoy the whole cupful in this measured way.

CREATE A PAUSE

You can do this exercise for the first
mouthful of any drink you consume
during the day – it's a lovely way
of bringing yourself into the
spaciousness of a single moment.

TIME YOURSELF

'Time is like a handful of sand – the tighter you grasp it, the
faster it runs through your fingers.'
HENRY DAVID THOREAU

Hourglasses have been around since Medieval times. We no longer need them to gauge the time of day, but we can use an hourglass as a time-management tool to give us the right sense of urgency and highlight the value of every passing minute. The fact is, you probably have more time and space in your life than you think. All of us procrastinate and fritter time in ways that do not sustain and nurture us – and the irony is that this means we end up spending more time on things we don't want to do, squeezing out the space available for those we do! Here's how to use the hourglass idea to tackle any task you are putting off, and so create more space in your day:

1. Set a timer. A large hourglass is a wonderfully evocative way to mark time, but you can also use any stopwatch device and set it to half an hour. When the timer starts, commit absolutely to your task – whether it is tidying the kitchen or reading a report – until the sands run out or the bell sounds.

2. At the end of your thirty minutes, take a five-minute break. Brains behave like muscles, both in the sense that they need both exercise and rest. A short rest or a change

of activity can refresh your thinking. Try something creative (such as doodling), physical (a short walk or stretching), or do some deep breathing or meditation.

3. Then reset the timer and repeat up to three more times – thirty minutes on a task, then a five-minute break. On the third half-hour cycle, take a longer twenty-five-minute break.

The hourglass can inspire us to use our time wisely. In this elegant object, we see the sand draining from one chamber to the other and know that it's a visual representation of the future slipping into the past.

THE HUMMINGBIRD

T he horizontal figure of eight — symbol of infinite space, time or quantity — is also a shape that occurs in nature. The hummingbird — uniquely among birds — beats its wings in a way that describes this shape. With their iridescent colouring and their ability to hover in mid-air, hummingbirds are much celebrated in myths of the North and South America, where they are found.

Finding the Light

Many myths hold that the hummingbird is a messenger to the gods and an explorer of other worlds. One story from the Mojave people of North America tells how early humans lived underground in darkness until one day they sent a hummingbird to find the way to the light-filled world above, where we now live. Another, from the Cochiti Indians, holds that the Great Mother became enraged at her subjects' lack of faith and removed the gift of rain from the world as a punishment. The hummingbird was the only creature to maintain its faith in her. When the starving people realized that the little bird was flourishing despite the drought, they followed it and discovered it had access to the underworld, where it could drink honey via a secret gateway open only to the faithful. They regained their faith and the Great Mother restored the rains. In all these stories, the hummingbird has the ability to move from the earthly to the sacred, inhabiting both spaces with ease.

SAVOUR THE SWEETNESS

'Gratitude is the fairest blossom which springs from the soul.'
HENRY WARD BEECHER

The hummingbird is known as the 'spirit bird' in the Native American and Aztec traditions. These beautiful iridescent birds flit from flower to flower exacting nectar. 'Nectar is sweeter within', is the emblem that the Hummingbird carries, helping us appreciate the special moments in life. Here is a mindful exercise to help you to enjoy the sweetness life has to offer:

1. Just before bedtime think about three things that you take for granted. You can include people, your own abilities or something else.
2. Commit to acknowledging each of these three things every day by vocalizing your appreciation to someone you love or writing it down. For example, appreciating the rain, electrical power, hamburgers, the lovely tree-lined streets or your supermarket that stays open twenty-four hours.
3. As you rest your head on your pillow, consider for a moment what life would look like without the things that you are thankful for.
4. Now close your eyes and inhale a dose of appreciation and exhale any stress that living without those things could bring.

5. In the morning, wake up feeling appreciative for being alive and all the wonderful things you have in your life. Remembering to get up with a smile and a bounce in your step is an appreciative start to any morning.

CELEBRATE YOU

A lovely way to practice gratitude is to take a moment each day to be thankful for your health and human abilities — such as movement, thought, and the senses: touch, taste, sight, smell and sound. Even if we are not in full health, we can appreciate what we do have and be thankful.

TAKE A STROLL

'In every walk in nature one receives far more than he seeks.'
JOHN MUIR

T ry using the idea of a lunchtime 'pilgrimage' to introduce a mini space into your day. There's plenty of research to show that going for a lunchtime walk is good for you — a study by the University of Birmingham found that it boosts mood and increases our ability to cope with stress. Turning your walk into an opportunity for reflection and mindfulness will give you a greater feeling of spaciousness and well-being. Here's how to turn your lunchtime walk into a peaceful pilgrimage:

1. Select a landmark a short distance from your place of work or your home. Choose something that is meaningful to you — a beautiful tree in a nearby park, a place of worship or just a building that you like.
2. Make a point of taking a break at lunchtime even if you are busy (perhaps especially if you are busy). Remind yourself you need the mental space that a short walk will bring. Then walk slowly to your chosen landmark. As you make your way, be aware of your surroundings, your breathing, the feeling on the sole of the foot as you take each step. Be as focused on your journey as on the destination.

A pilgrimage is a journey to a sacred space, and as one crosses the physical landscape, one also investigates the space within. The pilgrimage to Mecca, or the Hajj, is an essential duty all Muslims must complete in their lifetime – and is seen as one of the five pillars of the religion.

∽∾∾∾∾∾∾

3. When you reach your landmark, pause for a few moments and breathe deeply. Allow yourself to enjoy this momentary respite from doing. Then walk back and resume the activities of the day.

WINTER'S PAUSE

Winter is the Earth's pause – a time of rest and preparation that is necessary to make space for the fresh life and new activity of springtime. Many cultures in the Northern Hemisphere have myths that explain the cold months and the cyclical nature of the seasons. In one Scottish myth, a woman named Beira drinks from the well of youth on the longest day of the year and is thus transformed into the maiden Bride, who then gradually ages back into Beira as the months pass – a beautiful evocation of the cyclic oscillation between the colder and warmer months.

Persephone and Hades

But the most famous fable to explain the winter is the Greek story of Persephone. This beautiful maiden is daughter of Demeter, the goddess of the harvest. Persephone is captured by Hades, lord of the underworld and taken to be his queen. Distraught, Demeter removes her powers from the earth, letting the crops fail so that humankind goes hungry. Zeus, king of the gods, at first believes that Hades has the right to keep Persephone, but he eventually relents, heeding the pleas of the people, and rules as a compromise that Persephone will spend six months of the year in the underworld and six months above ground with her mother. Thus, each autumn and winter, Demeter mourns her lost daughter and the plants wither and die; when Persephone surfaces in spring, the world bursts into fruitful life once more.

HOW TO SAY NO

'Let us love winter, for it is the spring of genius.'
PIETRO ARETINO

Winter is a time when nature goes slow or seems to rest. It reminds us that all living things need times of inactivity, in order to prevent burn-out and exhaustion. But human beings are so driven, primed to overcome their own natural instincts. One result is that we often find ourselves agreeing to do more than we should, more than is good for us, simply because other people ask us too. But this instinct to say 'yes' can squeeze out the spaces that exist for us to nurture ourselves. Here's how to say no effectively:

1. Next time someone asks you to do something, notice that instinctive need to say 'yes'. Instead of answering straight away, take a breath — introducing a short space into the conversation gives you time to think.

2. Have a stalling phrase ready to hand: 'Let me check and get back to you' or even 'I'm not sure. I'll let you know'.

3. If you have instinctively said yes, allow yourself the space to retreat. 'Yes, I'd love to... but I will double-check and get back to you.'

4. Hold back on the reason. When we say 'no', we often soften our refusal with an excuse. This can act as an invitation for the other person to offer solutions or

MORE 'YES'!

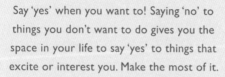

Say 'yes' when you want to! Saying 'no' to
things you don't want to do gives you the
space in your life to say 'yes' to things that
excite or interest you. Make the most of it.

arguments to convince us to change our minds, which
can introduce conflict into the discussion.

5. Mind your language. When refusing to do things, it's
better to use language that implies personal choice. One
study found that when people refused a salesperson's
pitch using the words 'I don't buy…' rather than 'I can't
buy…' their refusal was more easily accepted.

6. Have confidence. One of the reasons that we say 'yes'
is that we want other people to like us and approve our
decision-making. But when you get comfortable with
saying 'no', you generally find that others accept it more
easily than you would expect.

7. Practice. Take opportunities in day-to-day life to say
'no' without excuses or apologies – next time someone
comes to your door to ask you to sign up to a charity
subscription, for example, try saying 'I don't buy from
the door' with a smile before ending the interaction.

FOCUSED ATTENTION

I f you want to make space, commit to what you are doing. We are more productive if we apply ourselves to a task with a sense of focus – one that is as clear and targeted as the guiding beam of a lighthouse. And it is impossible to have a spacious mind when you are trying to do multiple things at once. Research shows that when we think we are multitasking, we are actually just flicking our attention back and forth from one task to another in a way that reduces our efficiency. Here's how to drop the multitasking habit and improve your productivity as well:

Do the most important thing first   Often we multitask as a way of procrastinating. Once you get a key task done, you can relax and enjoy ticking off the rest of your to-do list.

Create physical space   Decide what the essential tools are that you need in order to do a task well and pare down what you have close to hand to just these items. For example, if you are working on a computer, shut down any windows and applications that aren't necessary (especially your email).

Block off time   Commit to doing one task and only one task for a set period of time – and ideally find a space where nobody can interrupt you. Let people know what you are doing and ask them not to disturb you – put your phone on airplane mode, too.

Batch task   Switching from one activity to another very different type of task uses up brainpower. So group activities that are similar together. For example, if you have emails to answer, do a load in one go rather than answering them on an ad-hoc basis.

CREATING PAUSES

Rites of passage show the transition from one life stage to another – such as the progression from childhood to adulthood or graduation from full-time education to work. Ceremonies for this purpose occur in all known societies.

We can apply the idea of rites of passage to daily life, as a way of acknowledging all the transitions we make during the course of the day. Transitions involve ending one stage (separation), moving through (the threshold moment) and then arrival (embracing the new). We tend to think of our time in terms of our activities and forget about the times in between – but these transitions can provide us with pockets of peacefulness and space if only we can pay attention to them. Here's how to create a rite of passage to mark the daily transition from work to home:

1. **Separation** As you finish work for the day, have some small ritual that helps mark the ending point: tidy your desk, write a list of jobs for the next day, log off a computer... Take a deep breath here. Acknowledge that work is done, and you are entering a new phase.

2. **Threshold** When you arrive home, hover on the doorstep or entranceway momentarily: take another deep breath and acknowledge the fact that you are now passing into your new stage. Transition rituals often involve shedding clothes or cleansing the body as a way of signalling one's readiness to leave the past behind and

start afresh: when you get inside, take off your shoes or put more comfortable clothing on.

3. **Embracing the new** Take a few moments to arrive. Allow yourself to take in your surroundings and let go of the difficulties you have had in getting here. If you need to, close your eyes and take a few deep breaths, allowing your body to relax as you do so. If work thoughts intrude, have a notebook that you can jot concerns or reminders down in — the quicker you offload them, the sooner you can return to the reality of the moment.

MUSICAL INTERLUDE

'Lend your ears to music, open your eyes to painting and... stop thinking! Just ask yourself whether the work has enabled you to 'walk about' into a hitherto unknown world. If the answer is yes, what more do you want?'

WASSILY KANDINSKY

Music can take us to a different world and change our perception of time. When the mind is in a heightened emotional state, it is able to take on more information – and as a consequence time appears to pass more slowly. Paradoxically, the reverse can also be true: the mental engagement required when we are faced with something new and interesting can make time appear to pass more quickly. During the Renaissance, great thinkers believed that sound of the lute – a stringed instrument related to the mandolin and the guitar – could carry off the listener into realms of ecstasy. The Elizabethan playwright William Shakespeare makes several references to the special mood-altering music of the lute, which for him seemed to have an almost magical power.

Gassire's Lute

There is a West African myth known as 'Gassire's Lute', recounted by the twentieth-century German ethnologist Leo Frobenius. It is a story of an arrogant prince, Gassire, who is determined to achieve eternal fame through his brave exploits. He asks a wise man when his time of glory will come, but, to his horror, the sage tells him that his destiny is to play the lute. Determined to prove

himself, Gassire throws himself into a life of soldiering. He wins his battles, but in the process many of his soldiers die, including his own sons. The prince is so ambitious for himself that he barely notices these losses, but his people are outraged by his selfishness and indifference to their suffering. They come together to overthrow Gassire and banish him from the land. Alone in exile, Gassire picks up the lute and plays so beautifully that he feels both great joy at the music and deep sorrow at his errors. He learns that he will indeed find immortality – not on the battlefield, but through the power of music. It's a beautiful story that illustrates music's ability to bring us back to a space of self-awareness.

MINDFUL LISTENING

Today we are constantly surrounded by noise. Our heads so easily become consumed by our own inner voice, the voices of others and the myriad of sounds that fill our world. No wonder, then, that we often struggle not only to decipher what we hear but attend to it fully for more than a few seconds. Learning to be an effective listener is achievable with mindful practice.

Mindful listening is hearing without thinking; the idea is to be open to sounds without judging or being swayed by preconceived notions and memories. The exercise below challenges you to listen to a piece of music and to put aside any labels:

1. Find an unfamiliar piece of music. It could be any genre or artist.
2. Create a space free of distractions: it should be tidy, free of electronic devices and somewhere you will be uninterrupted for around ten minutes.
3. Sitting comfortably, take two cleansing breaths and slowly start relaxing your different muscle groups in turn, working down the body.
4. Take a few moments to take in the quiet that surrounds you and begin to empty your mind of thoughts, worries or judgements.
5. Embrace the calm that comes over you as you let go of your to-do list, mental cobwebs and 'ants' (annoying negative thoughts).

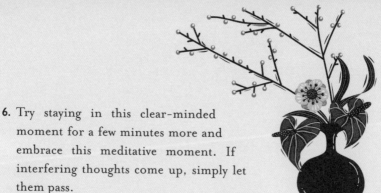

6. Try staying in this clear-minded moment for a few minutes more and embrace this meditative moment. If interfering thoughts come up, simply let them pass.

7. When your mind is fully relaxed and quieted, you are ready to put on your headset, turn on your chosen music and close your eyes.

8. First, listen to the music being completely neutral and trying not question the artist, types of instruments being played, what is about to come next, or any associations you might try to form with it.

9. Fully immerse yourself in the different sounds, tempo and lyrics. If your mind begins to wander toward likes or dislikes, redirect it back to just listening.

10. Become one with the music as if you were playing all the parts and singing all the vocals. See yourself on a musical journey, moving along to the sounds dancing about in your head.

11. When the piece is finished, gradually open your eyes and acknowledge that you let your mind relax while your ears did all the work. Spend some time reflecting on how it felt to purposefully diminish other distractions and allow your listening appreciation to grow.

WRITE IT DOWN

'I tell myself to throw the burden on my book and feel relieved.'

ANNE LISTER

When you tidy a room, you realize that things take up less space when they are placed in an orderly way. A list is a form of mental tidying – so that tasks and plans occupy less space in your mind.

Throughout history, great men and women have recorded their experiences and thoughts on paper, leaving their minds clear for their work. The United States' founding father Benjamin Franklin used his journal as a way to remind himself to make space for the positive qualities or 'virtues' he wanted to uphold in his conduct. Take inspiration from Benjamin Franklin and make your to-do list cover qualities as well as tasks:

1. Each evening, write your list for the next day. Keep your list to a maximum of three tasks. Long to-do lists feel overwhelming and are unachievable.
2. Don't feel that everything on your list has to be a major task. Sometimes taking clothes to the dry cleaners becomes a priority.
3. Beside your list of tasks, write down one quality that you want to bring to your day – efficiency, calmness, spaciousness.

4. In the morning, look at
   your list. Draw a circle around
   the quality you want to bring to your day, to
   help emphasize its importance.
5. In the evening tick off what you have done and reflect on
   whether you were able to express this quality at any point
   before writing your list for the next day in the same way.

ALONE TIME

Thinkers, artists and writers have long advocated periods of solitude as a way of creating the mental space that will enhance self-knowledge, understanding and creativity. Native American medicine men, Indian yogis, Christian nuns and monks... all have chosen solitude as part of their spiritual path. Psychoanalyst Donald Winnicott held that the capacity to be alone was a sign of maturity, whilst the eighteenth-century French philosopher Blaise Pascal argued that 'all of humanity's problems stem from man's inability to sit quietly in a room alone'. But still we find it so hard. Amazingly, one study found that most people preferred to give themselves a small electric shock than sit quietly alone!

The Hermit's Way

One of the strangest stories of a search for solitude concerns Saint Simeon Stylites. Born into a shepherd's family in the fourth century AD, in modern-day Turkey, Simeon became a devout Christian at the age of thirteen. He believed that austerity and self-denial were the route to spiritual understanding, but his practices were too extreme even for the monastery to which he belonged. He was expelled and went to live in a small hut. But solitude eluded him: crowds of people came to his hut, seeking healing, teaching and inspiration. To regain some peace and be alone, Simeon climbed a tall pillar where he spent his days and nights in prayer. In total he spent thirty-seven years up his pillar; the name by which he has become known – Stylites – means 'pillar-dweller'.

DIGITAL DETOX

Our digitally connected world means that our opportunities for solitude have shrunk. Even when we are alone in our own space, we can easily make contact with friends, acquaintances and strangers. This can be great, of course, but it also can cut us off from real-life experiences of day-to-day living. The average person is said to check their phone every six and a half minutes, a staggering 200 times a day. And there's increasing evidence that smartphones reduce our creativity – one study found that spending four days in a natural environment without technology increased capacity for creativity by 50 per cent. Here's how to take make time and space for yourself by taking a break from your smartphone:

Assess your tech life Write a list of all the gadgets you use and estimate how long you spend on each one. Then write down some of the things that you love but don't feel you have enough time for in life. This can help you to see how technology is eating into your leisure time.

Take a break Choose a period of time to abstain from using any gadgets. Start with ten minutes or an hour, whatever feels achievable. During this time, silence your gadgets and do something that you consider worthwhile. Do this each day until you feel comfortable with it, and then increase your time when you feel ready.

Don't be a message slave Switch off email and message notifications. That way you are not on alert, ready to drop what you are doing to respond to a message at any time of day. Consider disabling the email app on your phone. If you really need to be contactable, set up an auto-message asking emailers to call you if it is urgent.

Use an alarm clock Experts suggest we keep phones out of the bedroom because a smartphone emits 'blue light' that disrupts the body's production of melatonin, crucial for good sleep.

Wear a watch If you use your phone to tell the time, get a wrist watch to reduce the number of times you look at your phone.

Remove temptation Actively take up activities that mean you cannot use your phone – go to a yoga class, take up knitting, or go for walks and deliberately leave it at home.

Stack up When you are spending time with other people, place your phones in a stack so that you can give each other your full attention. It is a wonderful way to improve your relationships. Do this at mealtimes too, so that you can focus on your food.

Delete apps Delete all the apps on your phone and then re-download only the ones that you really need. You may find that you don't miss Facebook once the icon is no longer on your screen.

TAKING LEAVE

'The man who goes alone can start today; but he who travels
with another must wait till that other is ready.'

HENRY DAVID THOREAU

Getting out of the house can be one of circumstances in which we feel shortest of time and space: the taxi is outside, the train won't wait, there's no room for everyone to get their shoes on at once... Russians have a custom for these moments. It is called 'sitting for the road'. No matter how pressed for time you are, in the last moment before leaving the house everyone observes a moment of silence, looking each other in the eye, or sitting quietly if you are on your own. This creates space for meaningful goodbyes, as well as to prepare us for the journey ahead. Here's how to bring this custom to your own home:

1. Get absolutely ready to leave the home, with outdoor clothes and shoes on.
2. Then perch in whatever space you can find — if you are in a hallway with no chair, sit on the stairs or the floor.
3. If there are two or more of you, decide who is going to end the silence before you start — in Russian tradition, it is usually the most senior member of the family.
4. Then sit quietly, looking with kindness at the people you are travelling with and those you are leaving behind, allowing yourself this space to reflect on what they mean

to you. If you are alone, use this time to acknowledge
your home and what it means to you.

5. Once the silence is ended, leave the house in whatever
way you please: noisily, chaotically, hurriedly, lovingly...
You made the space and time; now it is behind you.

CHAPTER THREE:
A CLEAR MIND

*'Clarity of mind means clarity of passion, too;
this is why a great and clear mind loves ardently
and sees distinctly what he loves.'*

BLAISE PASCAL

JUST ENOUGH

The lovely word *lagom* is Swedish, and it is an idea that anyone who needs space in their lives should know about. *Lagom* means 'having sufficient'. It's the attitude of Goldilocks, who rejected Father Bear's way of being too much, Mother Bear's too little, but embraced everything to do with Baby Bear's 'just right'. Embracing a lagom attitude in all that you do can help you to feel more spacious and relaxed about life. Here are three key pointers:

1. **Satisfy needs** Most of us have far too much — we are always hankering after that new top, that designer kitchen, a bigger house, a better car. *Lagom* means recognizing the difference between what you need and what you want — and learning to be satisfied with less.

2. **Reduce your impact** *Lagom* is all about having a sustainable lifestyle, one in which you impact as little as possible on the Earth. So, try to avoid heavily packaged foods and unnecessary purchases; walk or ride a bicycle rather than take the car for short journeys; go for natural eco-friendly materials in clothing and furniture. Where possible, buy second-hand or upcycle things you already have rather than getting new things.

Lagom denotes an approach of gentle frugality and moderation, a way of conducting oneself that aims to create balance in all aspects of life.

3. **Be as well as do** It's easy to fall into the trap of believing you always need to be busy, achieving, succeeding. Our 24/7 culture encourages us to overextend ourselves and work excessive hours. Adopting the *lagom* attitude means being comfortable saying 'no' to engagements that don't appeal or serve you, and only staying late at work if you truly need to.

STORIES IN THE CLOUDS

*'Rest is not idleness, and to lie sometimes on the grass under trees
on a summer's day, listening to the murmur of the water, or watching
the clouds float across the sky, is by no means a waste of time.'*

JOHN LUBBOCK

Clouds are shape-shifting things. They can be a tiny presence in the sky, like islets in a stratospheric archipelago, or they can cover the blueness entirely in a blanket of grey and white. Either way, the wide expanse of the skies is their domain and they draw our attention to the vast space that is above us.

Everyone has had the experience of looking up at a cloud and seeing the outline of a face, a map or a monster. And when you look down on the clouds from a plane it is easy to imagine yourself climbing or resting on those pillowy peaks. Clouds make myth-tellers of us all, and not surprisingly they crop up in legends and stories from all over the world. In some ancient tales clouds stand for chaos and danger (when they are dark and storm-laden); and in others (when they are light and soft) they represent beauty and generosity — the source of life-giving water. Always they are uncontrollable, a symbol of natural freedom.

Classifying Clouds

The nineteenth-century Romantic poets were fascinated by clouds. William Wordsworth famously 'wandered lonely as a cloud', and Percy Bysshe Shelley wrote a poem in which a cloud represents the

endless cycle of life. The lyrical names for types of cloud — cirrus, cumulus, stratus, nimbus — were invented by a contemporary of these writers, a meteorologist named Luke Howard, in 1802. Nobody had previously thought of classifying clouds according to their 'species', as if they were plants or animals. Howard's work inspired the great German poet Johann Wolfgang von Goethe to write a series of verses extolling each of Howard's clouds. At this time, both poets and scientists were looking upwards to make sense of the world and their own place in it. It is a wonderful reminder that, when we need to make a little space in our lives, all we need do is to turn our eyes towards the heavens and watch the clouds go by.

PASSING THOUGHTS

Clouds inspire expansiveness: the wide reaches of the blue sky above us, populated by freely floating clouds that provoke the imagination.

Our lives are busier than we'd like to admit. It is easy to get trapped in the whirlwind of life in the twenty-first century and forget that our minds need space just as our bodies do. An uncluttered mind is one that has the freedom to reflect, explore and make important insights. Personal satisfaction and joy tell when our mind is unburdened and expansive. Try this meditation whenever you need to untangle your cluttered mind and make space for new ideas:

1. Place a comfortable chair in quiet area of your home or office. As you take a seat see yourself stepping off the crazy treadmill of life and into your mental space.
2. Spend a few minutes progressively relaxing your body, starting with your toes. Scan up your full body and, as you reach your head, close your eyes.
3. Imagine that you are now sitting up in the sky far away from your hyper-kinetic demanding life. As you anchor your awareness on your breathing, see your mind as spacious as the open sky in which you find yourself.
4. As you gently peruse your mind space, look out for any negative or worried thoughts.
5. Rather than judge that thought, try just to observe it.

6. Imagine that stressful thought as a cloud in the sky. Now try this with another thought and continue with each self-limiting thought that rises in your conscious mind until your sky is filled with white thought clouds.

7. See each one of your pesky thoughts clouds floating by you. Watch them transform into different shapes and as they gently drift out of sight.

8. Now accept that you are much more than your upsetting thoughts. You just found out that it is possible to get outside those thoughts and help them move on just like clouds in the sky.

WITHOUT JUDGEMENT

Whenever you capture negative thoughts try
to bring them to conscious awareness without
judgment. As you observe them, do not react
to them but allow each one to float above you.
Once you detach from your thoughts you can
choose to not get caught up in the ones that get
in the way of just being you.

A WISE APPROACH

I n these days of 24/7 news and social media, we are bombarded with ever-increasing amounts of information. But by ensuring that we pay attention to worthwhile sources, we can filter out much of the mental clutter that leaves us feeling overwhelmed. We can learn from the owl, which sits aloof and motionless on its branch until something of importance catches its attention.

Birds often figure in myth as symbols of knowledge and insight. The Norse god Odin was said to own two ravens who would 'fly each day over the spacious earth' and report back what they had discovered each night. Thus he was able to remain informed through the use of a trusted filter. We too can curate our sources to prevent information overload. Try these tips:

Seek out good sources Make an active choice to read a quality newspaper or news website. But challenge yourself too: read sources that come from a different political perspective than your own.

Go for a digest Just because news is updated constantly doesn't mean we need to be up-to-the-minute. If you want to stay well-informed, weekly news magazines can give you a deeper and usually more considered analysis of what is going on in the world.

Open to the arts Look at good pictures, read great fiction and non-fiction, listen to wonderful music. Works of art can convey timeless truths about human existence, but they require effort on

your part. Challenge yourself to read a great novel, spend an afternoon in an art gallery or to attend a classical concert.

Limit the unimportant   Much of the information we take in is forgettable and unimportant: we don't need to know what our friends ate for breakfast or what a celebrity is calling their baby, but we can waste hours idly scrolling through our news feeds all the same. It's thought that 30 per cent of the time we spend online is devoted to social media. If you want to stop information overload, quitting social media is the easiest way to do it — see page 88 for advice on a digital detox.

PERFECTLY IMPERFECT

*'It is better to live your own destiny imperfectly
than to live an imitation of somebody else's
life with perfection.'*

THE BHAGAVAD GITA

One of the ways in which we can constrict our minds is by telling ourselves that things have to be just so — exactly as we want them. Perfectionism is almost the opposite of spaciousness, because it means we discard or resist all outcomes except the one we had in mind at the start. The Japanese have a concept termed *wabi sabi*, which can be translated as 'flawed beauty' or 'the art of appreciating imperfection'. It is the antidote to pointless perfectionism.

The Art of Wabi Sabi

While Western ideals of beauty aim at smoothness, totality and symmetry, *wabi sabi* celebrates roughness, space and asymmetry. An artist might deliberately leave a corner of a painting unfinished as an expression of *wabi sabi*, in order to suggest that there is somewhere further to go, something more to be achieved. *Wabi sabi* also embraces damage, wear and tear, and repair — because it recognizes these things as reminders of the fleeting and imperfect nature of life. And so there is wabi sabi to found in things such as a chipped bowl, the clouded glass of an old mirror or a child's fingerprint on a once-freshly painted door. Or the imperfection

might be inherent in the object: a shelf made from driftwood, trickles of glaze on a fired pot or a rough-hewn slate fireplace. The point is always that flaws are an expression of beauty and truth. By bringing the *wabi sabi* mindset to our daily lives we can release ourselves from the need for perfection — which is generally unachievable and only serves to stifle our creativity — and embrace a more interesting, vibrant and open way of being.

EMBRACING FLAWS

When we are trying hard to be perfect, or when we will accept nothing less than perfection in our work or daily lives, then we cause ourselves stress. This inflexibility can also make us less willing to take risks – which can ultimately impede our success and our ability to expand our horizons. Psychologists have long known that there is a link between perfectionism and depression, but one Australian study has discovered that a certain amount of self-compassion can break this damaging bond. Learning to embrace flaws can help anyone wishing to create a more open and accepting mindset. If you notice that you are feeling stuck or stressed because something just has to be perfect, try this exercise:

1. Acknowledge your need for perfection. Even saying out loud 'I feel a need for this to be perfect' or 'I notice my need to achieve what I see as perfection' can be helpful. Take a few deep breaths and notice whatever feelings, thoughts and body sensations you experience when you say these words. Try to be open to their presence with a sense of gentleness and acceptance.

2. Recognize what you need to do. What will give you the best outcome in this situation? Do you need to prepare? Organize everything you need in advance? Get a good night's sleep? Write down anything that will help you to achieve your best in this situation.

3. Let go of the outcome. This is where the spaciousness comes in. If you acknowledge that your motivation is to achieve something, and you do what you can to make that possible, then that is your job done. Often an outcome depends on many things other than your efforts — other people, luck and happenstance, timing. Say to yourself 'I have done what I can, the rest is out of my hands'.

4. Then accept the outcome. Here, too, you can develop a sense of spaciousness. Say the result is less than you hoped. Can you — at least — accept that the upshot is what it is, rather than fruitlessly going over and over it in your mind, as if this will somehow change things? Be kind to yourself here. Perfectionism can sometimes mean pointless self-criticism.

5. Find the positive. Actively seek out the good things that are present in the outcome. Challenge yourself to complete the sentence 'The upside of this situation is:' and allow yourself to feel some satisfaction in what has been achieved. Sometimes you may need to be creative in completing this sentence — for example, one benefit may be that you have learned how not to do something.

6. Take steps to strengthen your capacity for acceptance generally — mindfulness meditation can help with this. Acceptance is a good counterbalance for perfectionist tendencies.

FIND YOUR FLOW

It takes great focus to create the flowing circular patterns of a Zen garden. As the monks work, their actions become so completely in harmony with the mind that other thoughts and feelings drop away. This meditative expansive state is something that we can access, not just through mindful action, but through any satisfying activity that absorbs us enough to create 'flow', according to psychologist Mihaly Csikszentmihalyi. A flow activity can be anything engaging – from making music to gardening. Here's how to choose a flow activity:

1. Make it enjoyable. Some people may get flow from playing the guitar, others from practising woodwork or cross stitch. It has to be something that you have fun with – a flow activity is its own reward. If there is an end result that is a bonus rather than the reason for doing it.

2. You should see results moment-by-moment. Flow activities provide instant feedback – if you are singing, you can hear the sounds you are making, if you are painting, you can see the picture take shape before your eyes.

3. You can immerse yourself in what you are doing. There's a balance between the challenge involved and your skill level – it shouldn't be so easy you can do it on auto-drive, nor so hard that it causes frustration. You want it to draw your focus so that your actions and your awareness come together in harmony.

A Zen garden is a representation of the wider world: its boulders symbolize mountains or islands, its carefully raked gravel the ocean or rivers, and any vegetation is forestland. And its beauty comes not merely from its carefully constructed appearance but from the process of raking itself, which Buddhist monks treat as a meditation.

⸻ ꙮ ⸻

4. You are unaware of yourself and of time. When you are engaged in a flow activity, you often lose any sense of self-consciousness, giving yourself over to the experience. Time often seems to pass more quickly — or occasionally more slowly — and your surroundings seem to fade away. All that matters is the task before you.

EXPLORING NEW LANDS

F rontiers mark the limit of settled civilization, beyond which is wilderness. The idea of the frontier is part of the mythic story of America, which glorifies the men and women who pushed westward into the wide, open plains. The boundless lands beyond the frontier stand for freedom, independence, room to breathe and grow. The romantic image of the frontiersman became a feature of American culture – starting with the stories of real-life pioneers such as Daniel Boone and Davy Crockett, and living on in the Hollywood fictions starring heroic types such as John Wayne, the archetypal cowboy. Although many now reflect on the cost of the frontier lifestyle, especially to the Native American peoples, the wild expansiveness of the West remains part of American folklore.

Wild Open Spaces

Many thoughtful Americans have used the idea of the frontier as a symbol or metaphor of the freedom that all people yearn for. Boone said he would 'certainly prefer a state of nature to a state of civilization' and nineteenth-century intellectuals took him at his word. Writers such as Ralph Waldo Emerson and Henry David Thoreau advocated spending time in the wilderness in order to find life's true meaning. But no one did more than Scottish-American John Muir to sing the praises of the wilderness. He walked thousands of miles through the southern reaches of the continent, choosing to follow the 'wildest, leafiest, and least trodden way I could find' and publishing an account of his travels.

OPEN TO NEW OPPORTUNITIES

'Wildness is a necessity.'
JOHN MUIR

The frontier inspires us to consider uncharted territories, pushing beyond our boundaries and planning new adventures. Here are some exercises that can be done individually, as and when needed. Each one can be used to open yourself up to new ventures and all sorts of exciting possibilities while helping you address any fears or anxieties that might be holding you back.

Be open   Reflect for a moment and ask yourself if you fully allow yourself to experience living or do you allow others/things to get in your way? The truth is that most of us have built walls up in fear of being hurt or rejected, or in fear of failure. It is possible to change that stance, but we first need to break through our defensive habits. Recognising when we are limiting ourselves is an important first step. List all the ways in the last six months that you have missed out on living, including trying new things.

Practice acceptance   Write down how others close to you have disappointed you. Next to each one of those judgments consider writing an accepting comment like, 'he never gave me verbal support, but I know that he finds speaking out difficult.' Fostering acceptance and letting go of criticism opens your mind up to possibilities in all sorts of creative ways.

Avoid tunnel vision   Note at least one goal in the last three months that you have fixated on in exclusion to everything else. Write down a date in the near future where you can put this goal on temporary ice in service of creating space to have some fun and freedom.

Drop the labels   Jot down two things that you consider unpleasant and two things that are lovely. As you look at what you wrote, think of the expansiveness and openness of the frontier where there are no negative or positive labels. Creating a world without labels opens us up to new opportunities and experiences unrestricted by pre-judgement.

Loose control   Write down three things that you try to control in your day to day life. It may be your diet, workout or a relationship. Now put a cross through each one. Control of people, places and things may give us a temporary feeling of security, but in the long run it limits our personal freedoms. Let go of control and you'll see things grow and change for the better in your life. If you picked up a beautiful dandelion would you trap it in your fist or let it breathe and fly away in your open hand? Think of your life this way and your possibilities will multiply!

HOLD STEADY

Meditators often talk of using the breath as an anchor — a way of holding yourself to the present moment as you explore the infinity of the soul. This exercise shows you a way of creating stability when you feel overwhelmed or stressed. It sounds counter-intuitive, but by focusing in on a tiny action you might find that you are able to open up to the experiences of the day. Here's how to do it:

1. Pick a small action that is unusual but simple to do — for example, gently squeezing the tip of one finger or tapping the fingers on your knee.
2. Take some deep breaths and bring to mind a time when you felt really calm and happy and spacious — looking at a sunset on holiday, walking through a field, standing on top of a steep hill you climbed. As you bring this situation to mind, do the action over and again.
3. Think of two more situations that made you feel the same way and each time repeat the action — the idea is to create a link, a strong mental association, between the action and the feeling.
4. Practise this daily for a couple of weeks. You can vary the scenario, but always stick with the same action as you do

An anchor is a way of creating a place of stability in the shifting oceans. Thus an anchor is an icon of steadfastness, of certainty in an uncertain world. An anchor also creates the possibility of exploration – of the self or other unknown horizons – because we know that we can strike out into the unknown so long as there is a way back to a place of safety.

the visualization. Then, whenever you want to access that feeling again, close your eyes and repeat the action. It's a wonderful way to return to a feeling of stability.

NATURAL PAUSE

Want to expand your mind and enhance your awareness of nature at the same time? Try flower arranging the Japanese way. *Ikebana* is more than a beautiful way with flowers — it is an expressive art intended to create a sense of unity and understanding of nature and of space, both in the viewer and in the practitioner. The minimalist constructions of *ikebana* may seem simple, but expert practitioners spend years learning the technical and creative skills. You don't need to do that to get some benefits — here are some basic principles to get you started:

Go slow   Approach the act of flower arranging as if it were a meditation. Take a deep breath before you start, and make your movements calm, fluid and aware.

Be spacious   Unlike Western flower arranging, which usually builds layers of flowers, an *ikebana* display is never crammed — you use as few elements as possible. The interaction between the different parts of the composition — which includes the vase — is what creates the overall harmonious effect. Each part of the arrangement should honour the others.

Think form   What matters is the overall effect of every part of the plant — the stem, the leaves — not just the showy flower. An *ikebana* is asymmetric — because perfect symmetry is not found in nature, so use elements of different heights, and angle your composition either toward the left or the right of the vase, not the middle. Always use an odd number of elements — three not four, for example.

Enjoy it At some stage, you may want to investigate the art of *ikebana* further, but for now feel your way into this new way of relating to nature. Experiment with different natural elements, vases and containers, shapes and styles and see what you come up with.

A PLACE OF REFUGE

An oasis is a desert island in reverse – a life-giving place of water amid an arid ocean of sand. So it is a space for both rest and refuge, one that defines the boundless wilderness all around. North African traders in their caravans would plan their treks across the Sahara by plotting a route from one oasis to the next, knowing that they and their pack camels could quench their thirst, and make ready for the next stage of their voyage across the high dunes and the dry seas.

The Legend of Huacachina

The tiny village of Huacachina, in Peru, is built around a lagoon that lies unexpectedly in the wind-sculpted landscape of the Atacama desert. A legend says it that a beautiful Incan princess was bathing when she was startled by a hunter. Horrified by the intrusion, she fled from her bath, grasping her cloak as she left. The folds of the cloak streaming behind her created the sand dunes that now surround her bath – the lagoon. It is also said that she returned later to live in the lake as a mermaid, remaining out of sight. Today the lagoon is a natural wonder of the country, and a picture of it features on a Peruvian banknote – meaning that Peruvians have a daily visual reminder of this wonderful place, even if they are far from it or have never seen it. All of us can use the image of an oasis to create a sense of space when we need to take refuge from an overcrowded day.

AN OASIS OF CALM

When we cannot find space in our lives, visualization can help us to access a place of serenity in our imagination. Try this beautiful exercise when you need a mental get-away:

1. Find somewhere comfortable to sit or lie down. You can do this meditation leaning back if you prefer, or sitting upright on a chair or a cushion on the floor.
2. Close your eyes and give yourself a few precious moments simply to sit and be. Breathe naturally and allow your attention to rest upon the gentle in and out of your belly as you breathe — place a hand here if you find that helps you to breathe more deeply.
3. Allow a picture to form in your mind of a beautiful desert, one with undulating sand dunes that stretch as far as you can see. The sky above you is deeply blue. Imagine the warm sun on your skin and the feeling of the sand beneath your toes.
4. Then, imagine that you are walking up a gently sloping dune. As you reach the top, you see below you a beautiful pool of water, fringed with palm trees — an oasis.
5. Build the image of the oasis in as much detail as you can — the glitter of the sun on the surface of the water, the rough brown trunks and the long green leaves of the trees. Perhaps there are cacti dotted about, some with gloriously coloured flowers.

A WELL-HONED TOOL

You can practise this exercise as a one-off, but if you do it regularly you will find it easier to access the sense of peace. You may like to have an image of an oasis on your desk or in your bag so you can connect with it at any point during the day. Some people like to record themselves speaking the script to use this as a guided meditation.

6. Draw closer now, and when you reach the oasis, find a place to rest next to the edge of the pool — perhaps shaded by the trees. Cup your hands to drink the refreshing water and really imagine the coolness on your hands and in your mouth. Perhaps hear the chirping of a bird or two or the hum of an insect.

7. Spend as much time as you wish sitting in this oasis — this blissful place of peace.

8. When you are ready to leave, let the image fade in your mind and bring your attention back to your body — noticing the contact between your body and the chair or sofa or cushion, becoming aware of your breathing once more. Then, open your eyes slowly and give yourself a few moments to take in your surroundings before ending the meditation.

THE SONG OF FREEDOM

B irds fly freely, and in many spiritual traditions they are a symbol of the soul. Caged birds, meanwhile, are a common symbol of constriction and imprisonment. 'The Gilded Cage', a painting by Evelyn De Morgan, depicts a wealthy man's wife gazing longingly out of the window. A songbird is there in the opulent room behind her, and it is clear that the occupant of the gilded cage is not only the bird but also the unhappy woman.

Escaping the Cage

Hans Christian Andersen's tale 'The Nightingale' tells of an emperor who prides himself on having the best of everything. When he hears of the song of the nightingale, he insists that she is brought to him. The little bird points out that her music sounds sweeter among the trees, yet she is taken to the emperor and entrances him and her court. Kept in a golden cage, the nightingale submits gracefully to her fate, but one day the emperor is given a clockwork nightingale, which everyone agrees is even better than the real thing. Noticing that her cage door has been left open, the nightingale flies out and returns to the forest. Years later, as the emperor lays close to death, his clockwork bird breaks down. Longing to hear the sweet birdsong once more, he hears the loyal nightingale singing outside his window. Her song restores him to life and, now wiser, the Emperor allows her to remain at liberty. The story is a parable that we can only be truly happy when we are able to live freely and according to our own nature.

OPENING THE DOOR

Old emotions and grudges can be like a cage, holding us back from embracing the positives in our lives. By practising forgiveness we can open the door and progress to better things. Forgiveness can be difficult, but it is important to remember that it is not the same as forgetting, nor does it mean that the person who wronged you should be allowed into your life. It is a way to release yourself from feelings of resentment, which ultimately constrict us. When practising this exercise, take as long as feels right at each stage of the process and feel free to stop at any point or to skip a stage.

1. Sit somewhere warm and comfortable, in your usual meditation position or crossed legged.
2. Take the time to relax into this moment. Focus on your breath as it passes in and out of the nostrils, and allow your body to settle a little more comfortably into its seat.
3. When you feel ready, bring to mind the person who has caused you pain, whether they are aware of this or not. If you find this too difficult, then you can use their name or perhaps a word or something that represents them.
4. Notice what happens in your body as you imagine this person – constriction in the throat, the pricking of tears behind the eyelids, shallower or more ragged breathing, tension in the belly... or emotions such as rage, grief or fear. Whatever comes, try to allow it to be – have an attitude of softness towards your emotions.

5. When you are able, imagine this person again. If it feels right, silently repeat these or similar words: 'As much as I am able right now, I forgive you.' Keep repeating these words and picturing the person – or holding the word or symbol that you have chosen to represent them – in your mind.

6. If a strong feeling or emotion comes up, you may like to soften around it, or it may be sufficient to gently notice that it is there and return to the phrases.

7. When you are ready to move on, bring your attention back to your breathing. Bring yourself to mind and silently repeat these words: 'As much as I am able right now, I forgive myself'. This may be for your part in the situation, other things you have done, for your inability to let go or to forgive as much as you would like.

8. To end the meditation, stay sitting and breathing for a few moments before opening your eyes slowly.

--- ∽∞∞∽ ---

GENTLY DOES IT

Don't worry if you do not feel any great wave of forgiveness – it can take time. If this exercise causes you pain, be gentle with yourself. Perhaps try doing the exercise again but directed at some smaller hurt. Sometimes it is worth seeking the help of a therapist to facilitate forgiveness work.

--- ∽∞∞∽ ---

PLACES OF SANCTUARY

S acred groves feature in the folklore and rituals of cultures around the world. There is something compelling about a tight and isolated group of trees that naturally disposes us towards stillness and reflection. There is a theory that stone columns, a feature of so many temples and churches down the ages, are more than an architectural necessity; they are actually stylized tree trunks, a subliminal reminder of a time before buildings, when humans gathered with their tribe in groves to seek comfort and meaning.

The Trees of Osun

Osun-Osogbo Sacred Grove, in Nigeria, is a sacred place to the Yoruba people, who once had hallowed groves near all their settlements. It is said that when Yoruba settlers first began felling trees, a voice from the water – the river goddess, Osun – bade them stop. So they left the trees untouched out of respect, and established their settlement nearby. In return Osun became the protector of their clan. In the 1950s, artists – led by the Australian-born Susanne Wenger – began to restore the grove which was threatened by encroaching farmland. The area became protected, while local craftspeople and artists worked to repair the structures and bring new works of art to maintain the sacred nature of the grove. Through these measures, the grove was restored to its role as a protected space for spiritual reflection and artistic expression. Devotees still come to pay homage, and each August there is a two-week festival that includes a procession to the grove.

TELL THE TREES

Spending time among trees has been found to have a therapeutic and restorative effect on the mind. When you are hemmed in by stress, it allows you to recover a sense of inner space. Forest walking can have a powerful effect on your mind and your body, according to a growing body of research. Japanese scientists have found that pine, fir, cedar and cypress trees emit substances that can reduce levels of the stress hormone cortisol in those standing or walking near them. Another study found that city dwellers who live close to trees tend to have better mental health than those who don't. So when your mind is full of worries, go outdoors and find your own sense of the sacred grove.

1. Go to the edge of an area of woodland. If you are in the city and it's difficult to get out to forest area, go to a park and stand at the edge of a wooded section. Switch your phone onto silent or turn it off altogether.
2. Look around you and find a rock or a stick or some other small object of nature. Holding it in your hand, take a few deep and calm breaths. Let whatever is worrying you surface in your mind and imagine that you are transferring it to the object – just for the moment.
3. Say out loud or silently in your mind: 'My worries and stresses are represented by this stick/stone.'
4. Then place the object somewhere you will be able to find it again – perhaps against a tree or under a large plant.

DECLUTTER YOUR MIND

We can allow our worries to take up too much space in our mind. Creating a physical symbol of stress allows us to put it down and re-encounter the spaciousness of the mind.

5. Walk into the woodland. Move slowly, allowing yourself to absorb the atmosphere of the wood. Engage all your senses: take in the colours around you, breathe the aromas, hear the sound of crunching or rustling underfoot as you step, notice any birdsong or sounds of other wildlife, stretch out your hand and touch the branches and bark... immerse yourself in the forest.

6. When it feels right, pause for a while. Choose a tree that appeals and sit with your back against the trunk. Close your eyes if you like and rest here.

7. Spend at least half an hour in the wood — longer if you like. Then slowly make your way back.

8. When you reach the place where you left your stone or stick that represents your worry and stress, take a deep breath. Allow yourself to leave it here, by the forest.

SILENCE IS GOLDEN

'Silence is the sleep that nourishes wisdom.'

FRANCIS BACON

In many religions, silence is used as a means of facilitating contemplation. Silence is more than a simple absence of words; true silence has a positive quality that allows us to access a greater state of awareness, connecting us with the space around us. Hindus call this *mauna* and it is seen as essential to spiritual understanding. Spending a prolonged period of time in silence can be a transformative practice that can help you to become more aware of the spaciousness of the mind.

1. Set aside a period of time for your silence. This could be a day, a morning or an afternoon. If you are new to the practice of silence, an hour is enough. Have an idea of what you are going to do: choose something that is generally calming for you – meditating, gardening, baking, cleaning – and have everything you need ready.

2. Ideally this is a time to spend alone, but if that is not possible, let anyone you live with know what you are doing. Switch off your phone entirely and unplug the landline. Also, turn off any other devices that emit noise (don't leave them on standby) – the TV, the radio, the computer, the printer. Cover any clocks, but set an alert for the time you want to finish.

3. At the start of your silence, spend some time in meditation or breathing awareness — you could do the exercise on page 112. Then go about your activities in absolute quiet, without speaking or reading or letting your mind wander into storytelling. Each time you change an activity or if you find yourself feeling distracted by thoughts or emotion, have a short period of meditation or breathing awareness to help you maintain a sense of reverence.

4. When your alert sounds, turn it off and sit for a short period. There's no need to break your silence straight away — allow yourself to transition back into normal life in a way that feels right for you. You may like to write a few lines about how it felt. It is sometimes instructive to do this straight away, and then again a few hours later.

FOCUSED MEDITATION

A mandala is used in meditation as a spiritual tool to connect with the universe. There are many different types of mandalas, but all are designed to capture and hold the attention. When we focus on a single object in this way, the mind quietens and we can encounter a profound sense of spaciousness within. Choose a mandala that appeals to you for this exercise — there are many that you can print out on the Internet. You can also do this exercise with a flower or other natural object if you prefer.

1. Find a comfortable and quiet place to sit. Place a mandala at eye level or just below it. Make sure there is nothing else around the image so that your focus is directed at the mandala alone.

2. Look at the mandala, relaxing your eyes to keep the gaze soft (blink as needed). Keep looking at it, allowing yourself to become absorbed by the colours and shapes. If you find yourself distracted, then simply recognize this and redirect your attention back to the mandala.

3. Start by gazing at the mandala for five minutes or so and build the time up gradually (set an alarm so that you do not have to keep looking at the time). Breathe naturally throughout. When it is time to end the meditation, gently release your gaze and allow yourself to slowly take in your surroundings for a few moments before you get up.

The term 'mandala' means circle, but the design is
much more than a geometric shape. It is a microcosm
of the cosmos and represents wholeness, perfection
and eternity. Tibetan Buddhist monks spend many
days painstakingly creating a mandala from sand as
a meditative practice, and then they destroy it, to
represent their ability to let go.

RELEASE YOUR WORRIES

There is something mesmerizing about releasing a lit lantern into the air and watching it rise up, higher and higher, until it disappears into the broad sky. Doing this is a wonderful way to remind ourselves of the infinite scope of the universe – which can help us to put our feelings into a wider perspective. It is believed that paper sky lanterns were invented 2,500 years ago in China. Some name the inventor as military commander Zhuge Liang, who used these floating lights like flares, to guide his troops as they marched through the night.

Festival of Lanterns

Many Asian countries have sky lantern festivals. In the town of Pingxi in Taiwan, thousands gather each year to launch lanterns into the heavens. The tradition is said to have begun more than 2,000 years ago, when bandits would raid the village, forcing the people to hide in the mountains. The village watchmen would set off fire lanterns as a signal when it was safe to return.

The city of Chiang Mai in Thailand has a similar festival called Yi Peng, which takes place in a full moon during November. On the night the sky is filled with lights. The ascending lanterns are seen as an act of worship to the Buddha – and it is especially propitious if a lantern floats out of sight. The lantern can be a reminder that we can – if we choose – learn to let go of negative feelings, and we can also use them to inspire us to express our wishes but understand the outcome is not always in our own hands.

LETTING GO

'Only from the heart can you touch the sky.'
RUMI

For centuries, Chinese lanterns have symbolized good fortune, long life, health and social status. If you are down on your luck and seeing little hope, the wish for a bright future can bypass you. Here is a visualization to help you stop trying to predict the happenings of tomorrow and let go of the need to fret over things you can't control. Let's begin this exercise by having you locate a comfortable place to rest your body and close your eyes.

1. Imagine it's the last hour of Chinese New Year and you have just finished putting your last worry about some future event or possibility inside your red paper lantern.
2. Red paper lanterns are meant to carry off our fears as they travel through the air, leaving us with a feeling of peaceful hope. Visualise launching your red paper lantern with all the thousands of others filling the air.
3. Track your lantern with all the others and see it disappear above the mountain tops and then out to sea.
4. As the gentle wind carries away your lantern, watch your anguish dissipate as you begin to reclaim a calm state of being.
5. Concentrate on the notion that life is full of uncertainties and that accepting the unknown is a natural part of living.

NO MORE 'WHAT IF?'

Try this visualization whenever you are 'what-ifing'. With practice you'll be able to accept that all your dwelling over the details of what may or may not happen next is just weighing you down and eating up precious moments for enjoyment.

6. As you come out of your visualisation, returning to the breath and gently opening your eyes, take a moment to consider how you feel about the worry that was troubling you. Are you better able to acknowledge that you can't always control everything and sometimes it is better to let worries go?

7. You can use the image of a sky lantern as a reminder of the need to sometimes let things pass. When you catch yourself fretting over some possible outcome or future event, simply close your eyes and bring to mind the image of a beautiful red lantern floating up into the fathomless skies, bringing you the mental spaciousness you need to step back from your concern and gain perspective.

STARRY SKIES

'This morning I saw the countryside from my window a long time before sunrise, with nothing but the morning star, which looked very big.'

VINCENT VAN GOGH

Cultures all over the world have seen patterns in the star-filled sky, and imbued the constellations with spiritual meaning. But you don't need a zodiac to understand or appreciate the night sky. If you simply gaze into the immensity of the night, and let go of the desire to label or categorize what we see, then you can actually create a greater sense of spaciousness and peace — one in which you connect with the universe without trying to hang a label on every twinkling point of light.

1. Go somewhere open, as far away as possible from houses and street lights — the darker it is, the more stars you can see. Wear warm clothing and take a picnic blanket or something to lie down on. Find a comfortable spot, lie down and close your eyes for a few moments. Breathe deeply and allow yourself to relax into the moment.

2. Slowly open your eyes and gaze upwards into the distance. Allow yourself to connect with the vast nocturnal emptiness above you, letting go of any tendency to identify particular constellations, stars or planets. Allow your breathing to follow its natural pace and your body to relax.

3. If you find yourself noticing, say, Orion's Belt or the Great Bear, close your eyes briefly before opening them again, letting your gaze become expansive and soft once more. It can be harder to do this than it sounds, because we are so used to categorising and labelling what we see. Maintain a sense of gentleness and be prepared to start the exercise over again, perhaps many times.

CHAPTER FOUR:
SPACE IN
THE BODY

*'Do not feel lonely. The entire universe
is inside of you.'*
RUMI

GREET THE DAY

The rising sun heralds a new day and is a symbol of continual renewal. The sun salutation in yoga is a lovely way to welcome the new day and open yourself to the possibilities before you. You can enjoy this simplified version at any time, but it's traditional to do it first thing, as the name implies, to greet the dawn.

1. Stand tall with your feet together. Take a few moments to find a comfortable but upright posture with your weight evenly balanced. Relax your shoulders, lift your head and then slightly drop the chin towards the chest to bring the neck in line with the spine.
2. Breathe deeply through the nostrils and bring your palms together in a prayer position in front of your chest. Focus your attention to your belly area, imagining that there is an inner sun here, radiating its warmth outwards through the body.
3. Breathing in, bring the arms up above your head, still in prayer position. If it feels comfortable, drop your head back slightly and look up at your hands. Then release the palms and turn them to face forward and comfortably (roughly shoulder-distance) apart.
4. Breathing out, circle the arms out to the side and downwards. Then, very slowly, fold at the hips to bring the torso forwards and then down, relaxing your body and letting the head drop down last. Your sitting bones

will move backwards to facilitate this movement. If you feel any strain in the lower back then bend your knees as much as you need to.

5. Rest here for a breath or two, letting the head hang. You can place the hands on your shins for support, or hold each elbow with the opposite hand if you like.

6. On an in-breath, lift the head and fold back up from the hips to return to a standing position. Breathe out.

7. Then breathe in and raise the arms above the head, before repeating the exercise.

THE BREATH OF LIFE

'There is one way of breathing that is shameful and constricted. Then,
there's another way: a breath of love that takes you all the way to infinity.'

RUMI

Most cultures entertain the idea that we consist of more than our physical body. Christian cultures talk of the soul, but in Asia and the East the concept of life energy is more prevalent. It does not denote the essence of the self; rather, life energy — termed *chi* in China, *qi* in Japan, *prana* in India — is the force that infuses all matter and all living beings.

Essential Prana

In one Indian tale, an argument broke out between the five faculties of man: speech, hearing, sight, the mind and the breath. Each insisted that they were the most important. So, to settle the matter, they agreed that each would leave the body for a period of time to see the impact of their absence. First, speech absented itself and the body became mute, but continued to thrive. Then the eye left and the body became blind, but continued to thrive. Next the ear left, and the body became deaf but continued to thrive. When the mind left the body became unconscious, but it continued to thrive nevertheless. So it was the turn of *prana*, the breath. But as soon as it began to leave, the body began to fail and all the other faculties felt their power weakening. So they begged *prana* to stay and acknowledged that it was essential to them all.

TAKE A BREATH

Breathing exercises are a traditional way both to bring energy into the body and to circulate it around the body. Many of us have a habit of shallow chest breathing, which causes tension and constriction, and so we need to actively practise belly breathing, known to promote calm and relaxation. On a physiological level, this helps create expansion between the ribs and between the hipbones, in turn promoting good, health-filled breathing.

1. You can do this exercise standing or sitting, but it's easiest to learn it lying down. Have your legs bent and your feet flat on the floor to relieve any pressure on the lower back. It's usually comfortable to have a low pillow (or a folded towel) under your head.

2. Place your hands on your belly, one resting on top of the other. Breathe out through the nostrils, exhaling all the air in your lungs.

3. Then breathe in, again though the nostrils, feeling your belly swell and gently push your hands outward.

4. Continue breathing in and out through the nostrils in this way, without pausing between the in-breath and the out-breath.

5. Then, try to visualize a small golden ball of energy in your belly, just below the navel. Imagine that it becomes larger and brighter with each breath into the abdomen.

6. Continue with the visualization for several minutes. When you are ready to end the exercise, let the image of the golden ball fade from your mind and let your breath settle into a natural rhythm, before gently releasing your hands and opening your eyes.

QUICK FIX

If at any point you feel overwhelmed or depleted during the day, gently notice whether your breathing is shallow or your posture is constricted. Straighten up, broaden your chest, place your hands on your belly and breathe into them for an instant refresh.

THE SPIRIT OF THE CAT

'There is no more intrepid explorer than a kitten.'

JULES CHAMPFLEURY

C ats have long symbolized independence and freedom. Although they are believed to have been domesticated 10,000 years ago, they still retain enough of their untamed nature to come and go as they please, shunning the confines of restricted space.

Freedom of the City

Cats were held sacred in Ancient Egypt, revered as honoured guests of the household. The Romans also held cats in high esteem, allowing them to wander at will through their temples (perhaps because they could not stop them). The cat was especially associated with goddess of freedom, Libertas, who is often shown with a cat at her feet. Interestingly, cats are still respected in modern-day Rome and have been designated part of the city's 'bio-culture' – there are some 300,000 living free in the ruins of the ancient city.

In all kinds of cultural contexts – high culture and popular, too – cats represent the idea of the unfettered spirit. The Impressionists included them in paintings as a symbol of their own artistic freedom; while in animal-based Disney cartoons such as *The Aristocats* and *The Lady and the Tramp*, there is always an indomitable, untrammelled, freewheeling feline presence.

'I value in the cat the independent almost ungrateful
spirit which prevents her from attaching herself to
anyone, the indifference with which she passes from
salon to the housetop… The cat lives alone, has no need
of society, obeys only when she pleases, pretends to sleep
so that she can see more clearly, and scratches everything
on which she can lay her paw.'

FRANÇOIS–RENÉ DE CHATEAUBRIAND

SPACE IN THE BODY

CAT'S BACK

Try this releasing feline stretch next time you feel tight in the body. Yoga can help us to occupy both our body and the space around us in a different, more expansive way, and can serve as a springboard for experimentation with movement. Try this cat pose – mimicking the action of a cat stretching its back: its gentle up-down motion helps to create greater space between the shoulder blades, within the ribcage, between the vertebrae in the spine, and in the belly and pelvis.

1. Get on your hands and knees, with your knees under your hips, and wrists, elbows and shoulders creating a straight line. Your fingers should be spread naturally, with the weight spread evenly over your hands, but let the palm lift slightly to avoid any sense of pressing. Your head should neither be dropped nor lifting, but in a neutral position with your gaze gently directed at the ground – it creates a straight line with the spine.
2. Take a few deep calm breaths, breathing in through the nose and out through the mouth, as you lengthen the spine and allow yourself to relax into the posture.
3. Breathing out, drop the pelvis and head, letting the back round so there is a natural arc from your tailbone to the top of your head.
4. Breathing in, lift the pelvis and head back to the original flat-back position. Breathe out here.

5. Breathing in again, raise your pelvis and head, letting the belly drop towards the floor and the back to curve. Look forwards, taking care not to constrict the neck.
6. Breathing out, return to the original flat-back position.
7. Do this sequence five times, working slowly and trying to maintain a sense of stretch along the spine. Then, breathing out, sit back on your heels to end.

───────── ○◦◦◦◦◦◦ ─────────

TAKE CARE

Use a yoga mat or a large towel to create a soft point of contact for your knees. Cat pose is a very gentle posture, provided that you respect the needs of your body, but if you have any neck or back problems, double-check that it is suitable for you with a medical practitioner.

───────── ○◦◦◦◦◦◦ ─────────

BRANCHING OUT

*'For in the true nature of things, if we rightly consider, every green
tree is far more glorious than if it were made of gold and silver.'*
MARTIN LUTHER

Trees occupy a much greater space than at first appears, because
their root systems can go deep down into the earth and spread
up to three times the height of the tree: these green giants live
underground as much as they do above it. Their size and majestic
form, their longevity, and their seemingly magical trick of coming
back to life each year, means that for ancient people trees were an
embodiment of eternity and the cyclical nature of existence. That
is why so many mythologies include a tree of life as part of their
cosmology – and why trees feature so often in literature as places
of magic and wonder

The Faraway Tree
One of the most perfectly realized fantasy trees must surely be Enid
Blyton's Faraway Tree. In her book series, three children discover
an enchanted wood near their home. One day they stumble upon
the Faraway Tree, a vast canopy laden with all manner of fruits
and home to a community of magical characters. Best of all, the
soaring upper reaches of the tree serves as a gateway to all kinds of
wondrous worlds – the Land of Goodies, the Land of Birthdays
and the Land of Do-As-You-Please – as well as the less-appealing
Land of Slaps. Blyton's magical world could be a modern version

of the ancient Norse world tree, Yggdrasil, which also reaches its branches into other worlds, in this case, the nine realms of the imagined universe. Across times and cultures, the symbolism of the tree still resonates deep within our souls, and can be used to foster the idea that the world is wider than we know, full of undreamed of vistas and undiscovered countries.

ROOT DOWN, REACH UP

The idea of rootedness crops up in many ancient mind-body practices, including t'ai chi and qigong. In these exercises, you learn to sink into the ground, like a tree holding fast to the earth. The aim is to give the body greater stability and strength, and maintain a sense of balance.

Rooting is a fantastic way to create a greater sense of space within the body, because it encourages good posture and elongates the spine — and it can also give you a better awareness of space outside yourself. Practise this exercise at home, and then try it next time you are stuck standing on crowded public transport.

1. Stand with your feet flat on the floor and shoulder-width apart; they should be parallel and facing forwards. Have a soft bend in the knees.
2. Drop your tailbone down and tuck it in slightly. Lift up in the spine and raise the head. Very slightly drop the chin, so that it is parallel to the floor. Place your tongue on the hard palate, just behind the front teeth.
3. Check that your shoulders are relaxed and dropping downwards. Have your arms hanging by your sides. Keep your hands relaxed, so the fingers are not touching each other but have small spaces in between them.
4. Breathe in and out through the nostrils. As you breathe out, imagine that breath travelling down the body into the abdomen and then continuing downwards, out

through the soles of the feet and deep into the earth. Imagine your legs and feet are putting out roots into the earth that the breath is travelling along.

5. As you breathe in, imagine that you are drawing the breath from those roots deep in the earth; drawing it up into the feet, up the legs and spine and out through the top of the head.

6. Continue breathing in this way feeling a sense of deep rootedness and connection to the earth.

7. When you are ready to end the exercise, simply bring your attention to your feet and notice the areas of contact with the ground before continuing with the activities of the day.

LEARNING T'AI CHI

T'ai chi or qigong are best learned in a class, though books and online courses are fantastic additional resources. There are many different styles so it is best to check out teachers in your area and sample the classes in order to ensure that they meet your learning style and situation.

EXPAND YOUR HORIZONS

P eople have always gazed at the horizon, the furthest point that the eye can see, and wondered what lies beyond it. The horizon was significant to the Ancient Egyptians because it was the place from where the sun rose and to where it set at night. The hieroglyphic they used for horizon was the *akhet*, in which two rounded peaks cradle the sun. Some scholars also believe that the looped cross known as the *ankh*, which represented life and immortality, may be a stylized depiction of the sun (the loop) rising above the horizon (the crossbar), while the straight section below represents the sun's pathway out of sight and towards the underworld.

Beyond Boundaries

For centuries the horizon represented the limit of human knowledge of the world. Before the age of exploration, ships tended to hug the coast and rarely lost sight of land. In the 1450s the Portuguese prince known as Henry the Navigator founded a nautical school in the city of Sagres, on the very southeastern tip of Europe. The school was a kind of research institute, dedicated to gathering all the information available about what lay out there in the 'unknown and tenebrous' sea. Once they were ready, intrepid Portuguese sailors set off to the west, passing over the mysterious horizon and out of sight, making their way (though they did not know it) towards the New World of the Americas.

BROADEN YOUR VIEW

'No borders, just horizons – only freedom.'
AMELIA EARHART

One reason we like to gaze upon the horizon is that looking at a broad view helps to activate our peripheral vision. Normally, we focus on what is right in front of us in order to concentrate; this is *foveal vision* and it is linked to the part of the nervous system associated with action, and also with stress. In times of extreme stress, we can become so tightly focused that we develop tunnel vision, in which we become unaware of anything other than a target. By contrast, our peripheral vision is thought to be linked to the parasympathetic nervous system, which manages relaxation. That's why looking at a wide, flat horizon can be deeply soothing. You can replicate the effect with this simple relaxation exercise:

1. Sit or stand in a comfortable but upright position and look at a point on the wall in front and slightly above you.
2. Keep your focus soft but keep gazing at this single point. Allow yourself to blink as necessary – it doesn't matter if you start blinking more than usual or not.
3. Then without moving your eyes, expand your visual awareness to encompass what lies either side of this point.
4. Keep broadening your visual field outwards until you are aware of what you can see out of the corners of your eyes.

FOCAL POINT TIP

If you find it hard to broaden your vision in this way, then use your fingers to help you. Hold up your forefingers side by side at eye level and focus on those. Very slowly move your fingers out to the sides and behind you, tracing the movement with your eyes until they are out of sight. This engages your peripheral vision. Once you can do that, try the exercise again.

5. Be aware of any changes in your body as you do this. You may feel your shoulders or jaw start to relax, your mind becoming clearer, or your thinking slow down. You may also find that you become more aware of the sounds around you.
6. And then keep going, imagining that your vision extends all the way behind you — 360° awareness.
7. When you have spent some time expanding your visual awareness in this way, look away from your spot on the wall and then re-engage with the activities of your day.

FLYING FREE

For ancient people, the manner in which a beautiful butterfly emerges from the confines of the chrysalis and flies off into the open sky must surely have seemed miraculous. So it is not surprising that the butterfly appears in myths all over the world, often representing transformation and rebirth. For the Ancient Greeks, the butterfly was a metaphor for the soul; in Japan and China, it symbolizes love and immortality. The butterfly was also an important animal symbol to many Native American tribes. The butterfly dance, in which young women dance with members of their clan, is a two-day ritual of the Hopi tribe that is both a thanksgiving for the harvest and a prayer for long life.

The Dance of the Butterfly

In one traditional Native American tale, a beautiful butterfly loses her mate. So deep is her grief that she takes off her wings and hides in a cocoon. But her friends and family keep coming to visit her until, unwilling to inflict her sorrow upon them, she departs on a long journey. One day, after many weeks and months, the butterfly notices that the stone she has stepped onto is warm and beautiful. The pleasure she takes in this tiny act of appreciation heals her heart, and she puts her wings back on and does a dance of gratitude for the opportunity she has to enjoy life once more. In this story, the act of dancing and the butterfly itself can be read as metaphors for the need to cast off old ways of being and embrace new ones.

DANCE FOR JOY

Dancing seems to be an instinctive action for human beings —
even small babies move in time to music when they hear it, and we
know from cave paintings and other ancient artefacts that societies
of all ages and places have enjoyed the ritual of dance. Modern
research shows that dancing can improve our spatial awareness,
helping us to occupy our own bodies and move with greater ease
in our surroundings. It expands the mind, making us feel more
creative, and it lifts the mood. If you are feeling constricted, either
physically or mentally, then dancing it out can be helpful; here are
some different ways to try:

Dance with a group   A study by the University of Oxford showed
that dancing with other people improves bonding, and it may be
that dancing — like singing — developed as a way of encouraging
groups to stick together. Scientists think that when we instinctively
match our movements to those of other people, we experience
'self-other merging' — a sense of fellow-feeling and connection.

Dance with a partner   Dancing is a great way to connect and build
trust with a loved one, especially if it is a form of dance in which
you touch each other. Partner dance, such as salsa or lindy hop, is
also a good way to increase confidence and widen your social circle.

Dance for fitness   A vigorous dance burns roughly the same calories
as an equal time spent swimming or jogging — and in a more

creative way. Dance also promotes good breathing and increases lung capacity; it improves stamina and circulation, and improves balance and coordination. So get moving!

Dance for release   The fluid movements of dance are a great way to express and release emotion. People who are depressed or anxious often adopt a posture of a bowed head and collapsed chest, but the expansive movements of a dance can promote a more open posture, which can affect mood for the better. There are dance classes specifically aimed at promoting emotional release — look for a Biodanza or 5Rhythms class if you want to try this.

Dance for confidence   There's something about the loosening up that you do when you dance that unleashes your inner power. However you move, use the uplifting power of dance to feel comfortable and strong in your own body.

Dance for yourself   Have fun experimenting with dance moves. Put the music on loud and dance around your kitchen. Try taking a movement that you perform every day, such as brushing your hair or cleaning your teeth, and turn it into a dance move.

Do a mini dance   If you can't get up and dance, try making dance moves with your fingers or toes, hands or feet, arms or legs. It's a wonderful way to keep the body moving and the circulation going.

FOOD FOR THOUGHT

M any religious and spiritual traditions encompass the idea of giving thanks before a meal. This same act of gratitude infuses the Christian custom of saying grace and Hindu chants recited before eating. It's a way of injecting a small pause of stillness so we can fully appreciate the food before us — and allows us not only to give thanks for what we have, but also to foster the relaxation in the body necessary for good digestion.

Giving Thanks

In Japan, the phrase 'itadakimasu' is commonly said before a mealtime — in a way that the French might say 'bon appétit'. It can be translated as 'I humbly receive' and the hands are pressed together, the head bowed slightly in an act of reverence. It encompasses not only gratitude for the food, but is an act of thanks to the bounty of nature and all those involved in bringing the meal to the table — the farmers, fishermen, transporters and shopkeepers, as well as the cook. 'Gochisousama', meaning 'thank you for the feast', is said after the meal, and again is directed at all those involved in gathering, preparing or presenting the food. Bringing this act of recognition to even a simple supper can be a wonderful way of turning a meal into a mindful space in the day.

MINDFUL EATING

'If the only prayer you said in your whole life was "thank you",
that would suffice.'
MEISTER ECKHART

Food is essential, but it is also one of life's joys. Mealtimes can be oases of pleasure and calm in the day. There are many ways that we can turn a meal from mere sustenance to mindful joy, and doing so helps us to eat what we need rather than overfilling the stomach. Practised over time, this can help you to reset your appetite and avoid mindless over-indulgence. Try these simple ways to introduce more mindfulness to your mealtimes:

Avoid distractions   When you eat, sit down rather than grabbing a sandwich on the run or standing up at the worktop. Create a sense of occasion by laying the table and presenting your food well, even – or perhaps especially – if you are eating alone.

Unplug   Turn off the TV and leave your mobile phone and other devices in another room so you can focus on the food before you.

Have a moment of pause   Stop for a moment before you start eating – instead of *itadakimasu* or grace, you may simply like to say 'I am grateful for this food' or a similar phrase.

Focus on a mouthful   For the first mouthful of every meal or snack, fully engage with all the senses involved in the process of eating. Allow yourself to notice the colours of the food, be aware of the movements your hand and arm make to bring it to your mouth, and then savour the aroma, taste and feel of the food in your mouth. You can continue to do this for every mouthful, of course.

Eat slowly   It's a good idea to put your knife and fork down between mouthfuls – this encourages you to focus on your food and digest properly. It also helps to prevent overeating: it takes up to twenty minutes for messages of fullness to reach the brain, so eating fast means you are more likely to overstuff the stomach before realizing you are too full.

The 80 per cent rule   Another tip is to eat until you are around 80 per cent full; this rule is followed by the people of Okinawa, the Japanese island believed to have the most centenarians in the world. Leaving space in your stomach is good for your longevity.

RESONATING WELLNESS

The sound 'om' – pronounced lengthily as a-ou-m – is held to represent both one's soul (*atman*) and the ultimate truth of the universe (*brahman*) in Hinduism. It is often chanted before and after a yoga session and is commonly used as a mantra, a meditative practice in which a sound or phrase is repeated over and over again. Mantra work is said to be one of the most universal mental practices in human civilization, and studies have found that repeating a mantra has a calming effect on the mind even in people who have never meditated before and who have no belief in the mantra idea. There may be a purely physical explanation for such results. A sound, after all, is a vibration, so when one pronounces the 'om', the word resonates through the body. It may be this sound ripple that induces a sense of relaxation, spaciousness and unity with one's surroundings. In any case, it is a fantastic and simple way to bring calm and spaciousness into your everyday.

1. Sit with the spine upright but not stiffly so. Cross your legs if you are on the floor or place both feet on the ground if on a chair. Place your hands on your lap.
2. Open your mouth wide and sound the 'aaaah' sound. Although the sound is created in the throat, you can feel the vibration in your lower abdomen.
3. Closing the mouth slightly, sound the 'u' as 'ooooh'. The sound will reverberate around the roof of the

mouth and the lips, and you will feel the vibration in your solar plexus.

4. Now softly close the mouth: the natural result will be a long 'mmmmm' that you might feel in the crown of the head. There should be a seamless transition between the 'aaaah' and the 'ooooh', and then the consonantal, humming 'mmmmm'.

5. Elongate the 'mmmmm' as long as you can without straining, and then take a breath in before repeating the mantra.

STILL WATERS

B athing is an art form in Japan, where people still gather at traditional bathhouses — *onsen* — where you languish in piping spring water. One of the oldest such spots is Dogo Onsen. According to legend, an egret injured his leg and bathed it in the hot spring until it healed and he could fly away. Noticing this, the people also took to bathing in the spring and news of its healing waters soon spread. Japanese *onsen* have a strict code of etiquette designed to help everyone experience a meditative bath-time and

create space in his or her daily routine. This exercise is a wonderful way to bring a sense of spaciousness and calm to your bath:

1. Prepare your space. *Onsen* are often outdoors in areas of natural beauty, and even the indoor bathhouses are elegantly designed. Make sure your bathroom is clear of any clutter and set the mood by lighting a few candles. Have a large bath towel to hand for when you get out.

2. Prepare the water. The volcanic spring water of the onsen is rich in minerals. Try adding bath salts or magnesium to your water, along with a few drops of a favourite essential oil diluted in a little milk.

3. Wash first. The Japanese always cleanse themselves before getting in the bath. Try dry-brushing and then showering if you have a separate shower, or simply washing the body with a flannel.

4. Lie in your bath and relax — no music or electronic devices or even books. Focus on slow deep breathing, or on the feel of your body as it rests in the water.

5. When you get out, wrap yourself in the towel and pat yourself dry. Put on a bathrobe and enjoy the time that the Japanese call *yuagari* — it means 'after the bath' and is a space in which you do nothing other than sip a drink and enjoy a moment of relaxation at the end of the day.

UNFURLING CALM

'The water-lily, in the midst of waters, opens its leaves and
expands its petals, at the first pattering of the shower, and rejoices
in the rain-drops with a quicker sympathy than the packed
shrubs in the sandy desert.'

SAMUEL TAYLOR COLERIDGE

The water lily, or lotus, is a perfect symbol of the act of opening, of expansiveness and dilation, as it unfurls its beautiful petals for the morning sun and gently closes them at night. Throughout history, the water lily has figured in stories and myth: it is an icon of enlightenment in Buddhism; in Hinduism, the water lily is associated with rebirth, the central concept of the Hindu worldview, and it is the national flower of Bangladesh, where it represents life and love. Further back, the water lily was part of the Egyptian creation myth: it was said that the god of sun, who banished darkness from the world, emerged from its flower.

Artist's Muse

Claude Monet painted the lily pond at his home in Giverny more than 250 times. It was the focus of almost all his artistic output as he grew older and his eyesight failed. The later paintings are mesmerizing close-up views of the water's surface; the flowers are painted loosely, with broad strokes, so the effect is almost abstract. Monet made a series of 12 water lily paintings that were intended to be displayed in a specially constructed oval room, so that the

viewer would literally be immersed in the work. The artist said he wanted to create 'the illusion of an endless whole, of water without horizon or bank ... the refuge of a peaceful meditation in the centre of a flowering aquarium'. He hoped that by so doing he would capture 'the variety and spaciousness of the world'.

OPENING UP TO RELAXATION

The progressive relaxation technique, developed in the 1920s and still recommended by health professionals today, helps you to learn the difference between a tense muscle and a relaxed one. That might sound pretty basic, but the fact is that we become so used to tightness and constriction in our bodies that we can prevent our muscles from loosening and lengthening the way they are supposed to. Progressive muscle relaxation has been found to improve sleep and alleviate conditions such as headaches and stomach cramps, which can be caused by physical tension. As you go through the exercise you may like to add in a visual cue such as the beautiful water lily opening its petals when you relax the muscles.

1. Sit down comfortably in a chair or on a sofa. Once you are used to the exercise you can do it in a lying-down position, too, but it is best to avoid this when you are first learning because you are likely to fall asleep.

2. To learn the basic technique, first breathe in deeply and clench one hand into a tight fist. Hold the tension for the count of five. Then release the tension as you breathe out. You might like to imagine the water lily with its tightly closed petals opening up into a beautiful open flower as you do this. Spend about ten seconds enjoying this feeling of release.

3. Repeat this tense-and-release process on different areas of the body, starting with the feet and working upwards.

4. First tense the right foot, squeeze it and curl the toes. Then push your right heel away from you, drawing the right toes closer to your shin to tense the calf. Then squeeze the right thigh muscle. Repeat all this on the left side.

5. Next, tense the right arm. Squeeze the right hand into a fist as in step 2. Then bend the hand up at the wrist to create tension in the forearm. Finally, raise the right forearm towards the upper arm, to tense the muscles here. Repeat on the left side.

6. Now start with the main part of the body. Begin by tensing the buttocks and pulling up on the pelvic floor. Then pull the muscles of the abdomen inwards.

7. For the chest, breathe in as deeply as you can and hold the breath. Then lift the shoulders high, up towards the ears.

8. End by focusing on tensing and relaxing the face: first, open the mouth wide, then squeeze your eyes tightly shut. End by raising the eyebrows high — as if startled — to tense the forehead.

9. Remember each time to hold the tension for the count of five, to release on a long out-breath and then to enjoy the feeling of relaxation for ten seconds or so.

FIND MORE SPACE

Within the pages of this book are tools, techniques and ideas that can help you to discover more spaciousness in your everyday life. To continue your spacious journey, try some of the resources below:

Books

*A Monk's Guide to a
Clean House and Mind*
Matsumoto, Shoukei, Penguin,
2018

Declutter Your Life
Hasson, Gill, Capstone, 2017

Declutter Your Mind
Davenport, Barrie and Scott,
S.J., Create Space, 2016

The Joy of Less
Jay, Francine, Chronicle, 2016

*The Life-Changing
Magic of Tidying*
Kondo, Marie, Vermillion,
2014

Websites

becomingminimalist.com
bemorewithless.com
simplefamilies.com
theartofsimple.net
theminimalists.com

Apps

BrightNest
Headspace
KonMari
LetGo
Sortly

Groups and Courses

meetup.com/topics/declutter
internationaldeclutterday.com

ABOUT THE AUTHORS AND ILLUSTRATOR

Dr. Arlene Unger is a California-based clinical psychologist and wellness coach, with thirty years of experience in the field. In her busy practice, The Empowerment Center, she emphasises the need to find life balance – and to let go of the judgement and self-criticism that can hold us back. She blends clinical expertise with her intuition and imagination, treating people face-to-face but also specializing in online coaching and counselling. She uses a wide range of therapeutic tools, including Mindfulness, Cognitive Behavioural Therapy and Emotional Brain Training.

Lona Eversden is the author of many books on well-being and happiness. She has a love of mythology and symbolism, and is interested in the overlap between ancient wisdom and modern science. She draws daily inspiration from yoga, mindfulness and gratitude work, which she has been practising for many years. Her published work includes books on mindfulness, meditation and yoga as well as dream interpretation and the art of rune reading.

Jo Parry is a professional illustrator and artist. She describes her artwork as 'fun, bold, colour-inspiring and unpretentious' and usually works in soft pastels. Her hobbies outside the artistic field include photography, travel, sport and cooking.

First published in 2018 by White Lion Publishing,
an imprint of The Quarto Group.
The Old Brewery, 6 Blundell Street,
London, N7 9BH,
United Kingdom

www.QuartoKnows.com

ISBN 978 1 78131 792 1
Ebook ISBN 978 1 78131 793 8

1 2 3 4 5 6 7 8 9 10
2018 2019 2020 2021 2022

Illustrations by Jo Parry Advocate Art Ltd
Design by Tokiko Morishima